THE

Endorsements

"If you are looking for a content-rich guide filled with practical tools and resources to cultivate your coaching excellence—you've come to the right place. Bruce is a leader among leaders who is committed to developing and empowering leaders. His book, The Coaching Leader, *is a concise handbook containing proven methodologies that have been verified and validated by the results they are producing in thousands of leaders throughout the United States and around the world."*

— Luke Laffin, President, Unleash Your Potential

*"*The Coaching Leader *will arm you with everything you need to become the next generation of leader that successful business will demand. It is packed with the why - what - how - who and even where to make it happen."*

— Jay Blanton, President, Jailbreak Leadership

"In The Coaching Leader, *Bruce has just handed every leader the playbook on how to help others win in life and leadership! The author's role as a practitioner shines through, delivering a wealth of wisdom and practical brilliance that can be applied in real-time. This book transcends theory, offering profound insight and proven tools for leaders aspiring to lead with impact and authenticity as they leverage the power of coaching to transform individuals and executives which will in turn transform their teams and organizations."*

— Keith Boyer, Founder and CEO, iNNOVO Coaching

"In The Coaching Leader, *Bruce Witt brilliantly captures the transformational essence of leadership through the lens of coaching. Drawing from deep insights and real-world applications, Witt underscores the imperative of fostering a coaching culture in today's dynamic organizations. This book is not just an exposition on leadership; it is a clarion call for leaders to truly engage, inspire, and elevate their teams. As the landscape of leadership evolves in the digital age,* The Coaching Leader *serves as a pivotal guide to navigating this shift, emphasizing the human side of leadership. For any leader aiming to amplify their influence and drive unmatched results, this is an indispensable read. A masterclass in leadership redefined!"*

— John Ramstead, CEO, Beyond Influence

"My friend Bruce Witt has captured the new rules for success in leadership. The old days of know-it-all managers and command-and-control leaders are dead. This book is a guide to greater team performance, increased employee morale, less turnover, and more fun in the workplace. The practical tools and principles in this book offer a clear path for leaders at every level, in any type of organization. You'll be glad you read The Coaching Leader *and that you picked up a copy for someone else."*

— Andy Wood, Ph.D., Executive Leadership Coach,
Organizational Consultant, Speaker and Author

"Bruce Witt is the perfect person to write this book tying together leadership and coaching. His principles and teachings are both rich in content and powerful in application. They are invaluable to both business and corporate leaders everywhere."

— Sam Y. Hwang, President of Hwang & Haas, PC;
President of Adoretech, Inc.;
Pastor, Christ Life Church

THE
COACHING
LEADER

MULTIPLY YOUR LEADERSHIP INFLUENCE AND IMPACT

BRUCE R. WITT

Brett
PROV 2015

ISBN: 978-1-7328200-9-8

Published by Leadership Revolution Inc.
Learn more at www.LeadershipRevolution.us

Copy Editing and Interior Layout: James Armstrong, UpWrite Publishing

Cover Design: Michael Sean Allen

Leadership Revolution, Inc.
Bruce Witt, President
4465 Nassau Way
Marietta, GA 30068
678-637-9890
Bruce@LeadershipRevolution.us
www.LeadershipRevolution.us

September 2023 Printing

Contents

THE COACHING LEADER

Chapter One

THE NEED OF THE HOUR

"The leader of the past knew how to tell. The leader of the future will know how to ask." — **Peter Drucker**

"The Great Resignation, the influx of Baby Boomers retiring, and the global pandemic have hastened the need for leaders to shift from the traditional style of 'telling' leadership to a collaborative, supportive, and interdependent view of the leader/follower dynamic. Now more than ever, leaders cannot assume that they know more than the people they lead, especially in regard to the unique expertise that each employee brings. Employees want to be heard and involved; they want to have a voice, and they want to know that their work is making a difference." — **Jay Bransford**

Today's climate of increasing complexity and change, the pace of technology, and remote workplaces have combined to significantly alter the direction and growth of how to be an effective leader. For a long period of time, traditional command-and-control styles of management and leadership, also known as "transactional leadership," were the way to succeed. Utilizing authority, power, and control, managers interacted with subordinates and provided incentives for good performance and consequences for poor performance.

Not today. Rapid, constant, and disruptive change is now the norm, and what succeeded in the past is no longer a strategy to what will succeed in the future. Today's leaders simply don't have all the right answers. To cope with this new reality, companies are moving away from top-down, command-and-control practices toward a collaborative, interactive approach that gives support and guidance rather than instructions. This allows the building of trust at all levels and empowers the employees to learn how to adapt to constantly changing environments in ways that unleash fresh energy, innovation, and commitment.

The Case for Coaching

In today's business world the challenges are significant: squeezing of profits due to sky-rocketing inflation, a dwindling workforce impacting employee retention, remote working that hinders communication and team performance, and lackluster incentives that fail to motivate people to increase performance. Effective leadership is what is needed to rise above these problems. Leadership behavior shapes 50-70% of organizational culture. In the same way, healthy leadership has a direct impact on organizational performance—including profit and loss, employee engagement, staff retention, and achieving purposes and objectives. Everything rises and falls on leadership.

What needs to change? What is working?

As leaders move from traditional boss to servant leader and on to coaching leader, the results are extraordinary.

"Companies like EDS, Chrysler and Herman Miller use coaching to create a culture of high performance, change and learning. Xerox, IBM, Microsoft and many others are training thousands of managers to become coaches. Executive coaches in New York, London, Paris and Tokyo are helping CEO's and senior and middle managers to unleash their unused potential for increased performance, satisfaction and results." — **Robert Hargrove, Masterful Coaching**

Michigan-based Triad Performance Technologies, Inc. studied and evaluated the effects of a coaching intervention on a group of regional and district sales managers within a large telecom organization. The third-party research study cites a 10:1 return on investment in less than one year. The study found that the following business outcomes were directly attributable to the coaching:

- Top performing staff, who were considering leaving the organization, were retained, resulting in reduced turnover, increased revenue, and improved customer satisfaction.
- A positive work environment was created, focusing on strategic account development and higher sales volume.
- Customer revenues and customer satisfaction were improved due to fully staffed and fully functioning territories.
- Revenues were increased due to managers improving their performance and exceeding their goals.

To be successful in today's ever-shifting market, leaders must value people more highly. People can make or break the best business strategy, and they can be the driver or the brake in adopting new technologies. People are not an implementation issue, nor just an operational or strategic asset. People are the raw resource around which business success revolves.

"No strategy, however well designed, will work unless you have the right people, with the right skills and behaviors, in the right roles, motivated in the right way and supported by the right leaders. Adopting new technologies without having the right people to use them wastes billions of dollars of investment by companies throughout the world." — **The Hay Group**

Case Study – Google's Project Oxygen

In an environment where the conventional is always challenged, Google's People Innovation Lab started Project Oxygen, trying to prove that manager quality does not have an impact on performance. To prove this point, they hired a group of statisticians to evaluate the differences between the highest and lowest rated managers. Data was collected using past performance appraisals, employee surveys, interviews, and other sources of employee feedback.

However, the results proved that good management actually makes a difference. To better define what makes a good manager they came up with a list of 8 qualities based on the data received.

1. Is a good coach.
2. Empowers the team and does not micromanage.
3. Expresses interest in and concern for team members' success and personal well-being.
4. Is productive and results oriented.
5. Is a good communicator—listens and shares information.
6. Helps with career development.
7. Has a clear vision and strategy for the team.
8. Has key technical skills that help him or her advise the team.

While this list seems obvious, there were three reasons why it had such a big impact on management at Google. First, it was based on people analytics. At Google scientific evidence is key; therefore using people analytics gave the project greater credibility. The fact that it was based on employee feedback encouraged wider employee buy-in and trust. Similarly, the hard data helped to convince managers why they needed to improve their management style.

Second, it was interesting to note that technical skills came in last. While it was important that managers have the needed technical level to guide employees, soft skills such as coaching and communication were absolutely essential. This proves that being a great developer doesn't necessarily make one a great manager.

Third, it provided a checklist of management qualities. As Bock explains in his book, whether or not your manager is well versed in management 101 and every training course your company offers, having a checklist makes a big difference as it actually prompts managers to remember and implement these skills on a daily basis.

A Case Study for Coaching - IBM

(as noted in a London Business School case study by *Harvard Business Review,* November-December 2019.)

Managers and professionals are busy people. If coaching strikes them as simply the latest fad being pushed by HR, they will roll their eyes and comply with the requirements as minimally as possible. If you want them to embrace coaching as not just a personal skill but also a source of cultural strength, you'll have to make clear why it's valuable for the business and their own success.

If you want the people you work with to embrace coaching, you first need to embrace it yourself. Nobody has done this better than Satya Nadella, the CEO of Microsoft. When Nadella took the reins in 2014, he was only the third chief executive in the company's four-decade history. During the 14-year tenure of his predecessor, Steve Ballmer, revenue had tripled and profits had doubled, but by the end of that time, the company had lost its momentum. A culture of inspection and judgment prevailed, and the managerial mindset was fixed: Managers evaluated direct reports according to how well they mastered skills and generated numbers that would allow them to reproduce the successes of the past.

This culture had contributed significantly to Microsoft's remarkable run of dominance in the world of personal computing. But as the energy in the tech sector shifted to smartphones and the cloud, the old management practices began to impede progress. By the time Nadella took over, risk aversion and internal politics were hampering cross-divisional collaboration, senior leaders were resisting open-source innovation, and the company's stock price had stalled. Additionally, technologies were changing so quickly that managers often had out-of-date knowledge and practices, but they kept passing these down because that's what they knew how to do.

Nadella quickly realized that Microsoft needed a cultural transformation. To regain its momentum and assert itself as a force in this new landscape, the company had to move away from its entrenched managerial style and instead develop what the Stanford psychologist Carol Dweck has called a growth mindset, in which everybody in the organization was open to constant learning and risk-taking. As Nadella himself aptly put it, the leaders of the company had to shift from being know-it-alls to being "learn-it-alls."

Nadella understood that the process had to start with him, so he began modeling the behaviors he wanted Microsoft's managers to adopt. He solicited thoughts from everybody he talked to and listened empathetically to what they had to say. He asked nondirective questions, demonstrating that his role was to support rather than judge. He encouraged people to be open about their mistakes and to learn from them. "He's with you," said Jean-Phillipe Courtois, a member of his leadership team. "You can feel it. You can see the body language. It doesn't matter if you're a top executive or a first-line seller; he has exactly the same quality of listening."

Modeling is powerful because it shows that a leader walks the talk. Moreover, it builds momentum. Researchers have found that when people are in doubt about what behavior is appropriate, they copy the actions of others—particularly those who have power and status. So it's not surprising that in these times of rapid change, which inevitably bring business uncertainty, employees look to their leaders for cues to follow. If they notice that their leaders are working to foster learning and cultivate the delicate art of leadership as conversation, they will do likewise.

Build capability throughout the organization.

After Nadella became Microsoft's CEO, the corporate climate changed and the company's performance surged. But Nadella was not single-handedly responsible. With more than 130,000 employees, he depended on the members of his leadership team to tailor the growth mindset to the unique requirements of their individual businesses. For

Courtois—who in 2016 assumed control of Microsoft's global sales, marketing, and operations—that meant transforming the culture from one of command and control to one of coaching.

Courtois recognized that the "why" of the shift to coaching was Microsoft's move to a cloud-first strategy. The fundamental economics of cloud computing is based on the premise that customers will pay only for the resources they use (how long a server is utilized, say, or how much data bandwidth is being consumed). With revenue growth now depending more heavily on the consumption of Microsoft's offerings, everyone at the company had to become adept at having conversations in which they could learn what they did not already know—how to serve the unmet needs of their customers. And with the availability of powerful digital tools that provided everyone with real-time data on key metrics, it no longer made sense for managers to spend their time monitoring and controlling employees. So, after a restructuring effort aimed at giving Microsoft's sales teams the right technical and industry skills to accompany corporate customers as they moved to the cloud, Courtois followed up with workshops, tools, and an online course designed to help the company's managers develop a coaching style of leadership.

"If we want to get the transformation all the way through the organization," he told us, "our biggest challenge is to reboot our people managers. 'People manager' is a job. You're not just a sales manager, where you have a quota, a territory, customers, partners, and goals to achieve. You're actually someone whose mission it is to pick, grow, and motivate the best capabilities to build customer success."

Over time, the midyear review had developed into a kind of corporate theater in which the C-suite team, adopting an interrogatory stance, would grill senior managers from around the world on their progress and plans. This format of "precision questioning" ended up having "a fear impact on people," said one executive, "because they felt like they were going into that meeting to be judged personally. So they felt they had to paint the best picture they could without showing any mistakes or failures." Stories abounded of senior managers anxiously beginning their preparation well before the December holiday period. In other words, to make a good impression, a raft of the company's most valuable people were diverting more than a month of their time to preparing for an internal review.

As part of the shift to a learning culture, Courtois had already encouraged his team to abandon precision questioning in favor of a more coaching-oriented approach that involved asking questions such as "What are you trying to do?" "What's working?" "What's not working?" and "How can we help?" But old habits die hard. Only after Courtois eliminated the midyear review—thereby removing a significant barrier to change—did everybody understand that he meant business.

The Role of the Coaching Leader

The Coaching Leader at the core produces conversations that produce results and success. This is a collaborative work between a leader, individuals, and teams that boosts productivity, engagement, commitment, and results. By utilizing the elements of the coaching process, you will engage in a repeatable process that helps both the leader and the individual. This process combines strength and toughness, courage and tenacity, and heart and kindness. It treats individuals as people who have dreams, desires, and a life outside of work, while also expecting a commitment, hard work, and responsibility.

"This is a dramatic and fundamental shift, and we've observed it firsthand. Over the past decade, we've seen it in our ongoing research on how organizations are transforming themselves for the digital age; we've discerned it from what our executive students and coaching clients have told us about the leadership skills they want to cultivate in themselves and throughout their firms, and we've noticed that more and more of the companies we work with

are investing in training their leaders as coaches. Increasingly, coaching is becoming integral to the fabric of a learning culture—a skill that good managers at all levels need to develop and deploy."
— ***Harvard Business Review,*** **November-December 2019**

Every leader wants to help their direct reports to do better. But when they're asked to role-play a coaching conversation with them, they demonstrate much room for improvement. They know what they're supposed to do: "ask and listen," not "tell and sell." But that doesn't come naturally, because deep down they've already made up their minds about the right way forward, usually before they even begin talking to the employee. So their efforts to coach typically consist of just trying to get an agreement on what they've already decided. That's not real coaching—and not surprisingly, it doesn't play out well.

This is where coaching plays a key role in the future of leadership.

Summary

As the leader, you can change the culture by embracing this coaching approach to leadership. Your influence will grow, your people will be empowered, and they will execute with greater engagement. This all can and will translate into having a greater influence and multiplying the impact of the organization.

The Benefits and Outcomes of a Coaching Leader

- Dramatically changes the culture and achieves increased organizational alignment.
- Develops personal leadership and internal leadership bench strength.
- Brings higher levels of employee commitment, retention, and engagement.
- Focuses on excellence and greater accountability for performance that yields greater results.
- Improves your team's function and health.

Chapter Two

PRINCIPLES AND BEST PRACTICES OF THE COACHING LEADER

Coaching Overview

The coaching process, when done well, results in greater impact, leaders being developed, and a more cohesive culture. Coaching is the one thing that will move the needle faster and farther than most any other skill set. As we embark on this process of understanding coaching and developing skills around coaching, we will see that it creates the following outcomes:

- Clarity around personal goals, team engagement, and organizational effectiveness.
- Strategic planning that is comprehensive and actionable.
- Leaders mastering their mindset.
- Upgrading the leader's skill in coaching.
- Optimizing communication, operations, and decision making.
- Focusing priorities and strengths.
- Optimizing the leader's time and talents.
- Scaling results and outcomes.
- Unlocking the "What is Next?" question.
- Making a lasting impact.

The Coaching Leader Principles

"When we help ourselves, we find moments of happiness. When we help others, we find lasting fulfillment." — **Simon Sinek**

"You can have everything in life you want if you will just help enough other people get what they want." — **Zig Ziglar**

"Leadership is not about you; it's about investing in the growth of others." — **Ken Blanchard**

The coaching leader recognizes they have the ultimate responsibility to lead and guide the people, and thus the organization, to greater results. As already mentioned, the leader who practices the skills of coaching blends strength and toughness, courage and tenacity, and heart and kindness. At the core of this is the belief and action that the people matter; it is not just about the results. Thus, the foundational principle of coaching is "life on life."

Life on Life Principles

- Patience on the coach's part. Don't try to fix people. Don't over-direct them. Help them make wise decisions.
- Be a life coach—ask good questions and listen. Care for the person.
- Believe the best about the individual. Be an encourager. Instill hope.
- Goals don't equal outcome—priorities always equal outcome.
- The process is as important as the product. Develop thinking and taking responsibility.

Things to Guard Against

- Projecting your way; being too quick to judge or give answers.
- Telling the answer upfront. People want to discover and not be told. Model the answer, don't talk about it. Don't give too much information. You can tell stories, yet don't talk about yourself too much.
- Focused solely on performance. Be careful not to impugn motive unless there is a clear reason.
- Don't just focus on the bottom line. People want relationships and connections marked by vulnerability and authenticity. They want to hear stories of challenges as well as good.

- Everyone can be too busy. Employees often aren't asking questions because it takes more time. We need to do more listening, so keep asking. Don't have answers to questions they are not asking.
- Don't fight the failures, learn from them; they produce growth. Don't always talk about victories and overlook failures. Victories build walls, failure builds bridges.

The Goal of the Coaching Leader

Help your people develop a proper mindset of thinking about Purpose, Perspective, Responsibility, and Execution.

Five Focus Areas of The Coaching Leader

1. **Focus on principles before the product.** The end does not justify the means. Bigger is not better. The process is equal to the product—motive is as important as the outcome.
2. **Focus on character before competence.** Intelligence without character will kill you.
3. **Focus on taking responsibility rather than removing problems.** A pain-free life is a fantasy.
4. **Focus on developing thinking rather than techniques.** Start with why and how follows.
5. **Focus on function before form.** Don't be enamored or married to the form. Be careful of measuring the activity. Don't confuse activity for productivity; don't confuse productivity for reproductivity.

The Coaching Leader's Best Practices

"If you look over people in your business life, you are a coach. Face it. You may hide behind a title like a manager, VP, or director—but in the end, if you aren't a coach then no one will follow you."
— Tim Sanders, former Chief Solutions Officer at Yahoo!

15

The Future of Leadership Emphasizes Coaching

A leadership coach is a person who primarily uses questions to help another person identify a goal and actions to take, build commitment, offer accountability, follow up on progress, and ultimately help someone to successfully change. Coaching is not teaching, offering advice, suggesting, or setting goals on someone else's behalf. It is also not taking responsibility to "fix" someone. Instead, a coach believes in the person and in God's ability to work in and through him/her and his/her stakeholders to bring about the desired change.

Coaches are:

- Relational and Supportive.
- Trusting and Focused.
- Curious and Goal-oriented.
- Observant and Respectful.
- Listeners and Powerful questioners.

Coaching is a skill set of effective leaders that can be learned. The basic premise of coaching is asking questions. As leaders, it's tempting to tell our employees exactly what to do—telling often saves time and ensures the desired outcome. However, by asking questions, coaching provides opportunities for employees to come up with solutions on their own. This allows them to be interdependent and committed to the outcome. Coaching requires patience and discipline, but the long-term advantages outweigh the momentary inconvenience. Of course, there will be times when a leader needs to be directive or corrective; good leaders know when coaching is appropriate.

The Coaching Leader Made Practical and Powerful with Best Practices

1. Coaching Framework

Coaching is a relational change process that helps transform leaders and people. Coaching is a relationship of trust, authenticity, care, belief, and accountability. Coaching is a process of both context and conversation that

16

focuses on purpose, planning, execution, and skill development.

2. *Coaching Made Simple*

Coaching facilitates change. Change happens when we are motivated to change and act on it, especially when there is a healthy process for change.

Why – Coaching provides meaningful support, personal encouragement, and transformation.

Who – Coaching is about helping others achieve their goals and plans.

What – Coaching is an exploring, learning, and discovery process in the context of a relationship that seeks the personal growth of the individual in order to problem-solve and execute.

How – Coaching simply exercises listening to the heart, asking powerful questions, clarifying key action steps, and holding each person accountable.

3. *Coaching Values*

The coaching relationship and process are based on a set of core values that must be embraced, lived, and modeled. Values direct behavior, and without values the behavior has no anchor. The key value is "Believing the Best." That involves believing the best in the person, helping the person be their best, and expecting the best of the person.

4. *Coaching Leadership Begins with a Trust Relationship.*

An effective coaching leader works hard at developing a relationship with the coachee as this is fundamental to all that follows. This relationship is characterized by trust. Without trust and a relationship, there will be very little lasting change or results.

Coaching Fundamental Skill Sets

Effective leaders not only know how to guide a discussion and interaction, but they have developed the skill of coaching or drawing out of a person directions, insights, and thoughts that prove invaluable to the one being coached. Four Key Fundamentals form the foundation of this coaching skill: Active Listening, Powerful Questions, Goal Setting, and Accountability.

1. Active Listening

The first foundational skill in coaching is listening well, or active listening. Listening is a skill that engages both the coach and coachee in a relationship of understanding and communicates value and interest to the coachee.

"A coach is an active listener—having the ability to focus completely on what the coachee is saying and not saying—not passively absorbing what is being said, but intentionally and intuitively grasping the facts and feelings inherent in what he is hearing."
— Center for the Advancement of Christian Coaching

This type of listening creates an environment of trust, value, and safety. This allows the coachee to open up and express his or her thoughts and explore many alternatives. It helps to bring to the surface issues that might not normally come up. By this type of intentional listening, the coachee wants to participate and grow in the relationship. Conversely, if the coachees do not feel listened to, they will begin to shut down.

Why is listening difficult?

How can you improve your listening skills?

2. Powerful Questions

Active listening is one of three major disciplines used in coaching. The second is closely related to it: the ability to ask insightful or powerful questions. Powerful questions are open-ended often probing questions that help the coachee to open up, be vulnerable, and to look at the situation from a new perspective.

Powerful questions are used for many different purposes:
- Draw out new ideas, thoughts, reflections, and conclusions.
- Aid in understanding or unpacking an issue or thought.
- Help a coachee to dig deeper in examining an idea or thought.
- Check for commitment to an action step.
- Discern understanding or clarification.

Understanding what kinds of questions not to ask is a great aid in choosing the best questions.

Questions to avoid:

- Leading Questions: questions that suggest a path of action or an answer that you as the coach would like to interject into the conversation. Leading questions take responsibility away from the coachee as the coach sets the agenda for the conversation. For example, don't begin questions with, *"Wouldn't you agree that…?"*

- Closed Questions: questions that can be answered with a simple "yes" or "no." Closed questions don't cause the coachee to think creatively.

- For example, instead of asking, *"Have you thought about confronting your employee?"* ask, *"If necessary, what would be the most productive way to confront your employee?"*

- Judgmental Questions: questions that contain an explicit or implicit statement of the coach's negative opinion of the coachee. Example, *"What caused you to totally neglect your employee?"*

- Advice Questions: questions that are really advice with a question mark tacked on to the end of the sentence. Example: *"Have you considered confronting your employee?"* Translation: *"You need to confront your employee."*

- Why Questions: questions that contain the word "why." The word "why" often causes a defensive response. Example: *"Why didn't you finalize the sales report on time?"*

Why are questions so important for a leader? How can you use more questions rather than telling someone what to do?

3. *Goal Setting*

Goal setting is the process of defining where, what, and how you want to proceed in a certain direction for both personal and career opportunities. Goal setting begins with having a picture/vision of where you are going. A coaching leader helps the person capture this process for themselves. The GROW model helps guide a person.

G – Goal or end game. What does success look like?

R – Reality

O – Options, opportunities, obstacles

W – What steps will you take?

Goal setting involves two key steps: 1) crafting and writing out a goal, and 2) formulating specific strategies and action steps to reach that goal. Coaching revolves around goals that the coachee brings to the relationship, or that the coach helps the coachee to create. Setting and pursuing effective and realistic goals in any area is what makes coaching a forward-moving, growth-oriented process.

Many times, however, the goal-setting process is hampered by a lack of clear goals or just wishful desires. It is common for a coachee to set a goal that is likely to fail because it cannot be measured, or it is so broad or general that the coachee has no idea how to begin working on it. The SMART goal pattern is a tool coaches can use to help coachees establish goals that will truly result in change and growth in their life. SMART goals are:

Specific: Clear, concrete, and with detail.

"I want to work harder at work" is not specific.

"I want to improve my job performance by being accountable on a weekly basis" is specific.

Without specificity, a goal can never truly be reached.

Measurable: Progress can be quantified or objectified and measured.

"I want to grow my territory" is not measurable.

"I want to increase my sales by 10%" is measurable.

An effective goal requires a statement of the tangible evidence that it's been reached.

Attainable: Challenging and compelling, yet doable.

"I will be the top salesperson in my industry" may not be immediately attainable.

"I will be the top salesperson in my division" may be more attainable.

If a goal requires a person to adapt far outside of his or her true self, it will become burdensome and ultimately demotivating. However, it should be challenging enough to cause a person to have to stretch to achieve it.

Relevant: Meaningful and important.

"I want my family to be debt-free by 2024" is relevant to a man who highly values debt-free living.

"I will grow production capabilities by 25% to prepare the new product we are introducing next year" is relevant because the capacity precedes the selling of a new product. Goals that are explicitly connected to core values or sales will be highly motivational to the process.

Time specific: Includes a beginning and ending point.

"I think I'd like to complete the project in the next few months" is not time specific.

"I will complete the project by February 15" is time specific.

Attaching start and end dates provides the "race-track" needed to keep a person on course with a clear finish line.

GROW Model – Identify the issue. This model is a simple guide to developing a plan.

G – Goal	What is your desired goal and outcome?
R – Reality	What is your current reality? Where are you today?
O – Opportunities	What are the opportunities?
Options	What are the possible options?
Obstacles	What are the obstacles, barriers, or roadblocks?
W – What	What action steps will you take?

Self-reflecting questions:

- Which of the above techniques do you need to apply in your own coaching roles?

- Which do you intuitively do better than the others?

- What benefits could you realize in your coaching role(s) by using SMART coaching?

4. *Accountability – Inspect What You Expect*

Accountability is one of the great challenges and opportunities for a leader in business. Too often we feel uncomfortable holding others accountable or don't like being held to account ourselves.

Teams and people that do not hold one another accountable…

- Create resentment among team members who have different standards of performance.
- Encourage mediocrity.
- Miss deadlines and key deliverables.

Accountability is the process of giving a report or furnishing an explanation of responsibility about a project or situation to achieve an agreed-upon result.

Accountability can be a great asset in helping teams and organizations flourish and succeed. It is fundamental to teamwork. Accountability means the willingness of team members to remind one another when they are not living up to agreed-on performance standards. The golden rule of management is **"what gets measured gets completed."** This is accountability.

The key to making accountability part of a team's culture is the willingness of the team leader to model the behavior by stepping right into the middle of a difficult situation. This will serve to remind team members of their responsibilities, behavior, and results. Although, the leader should not be the only source of accountability, they should be the ultimate source.

The key is to overcome the reluctance to give one another critical feedback. The most effective way to overcome this reluctance is to help people realize that failing to provide peers with constructive feedback means that they are letting them down personally. By holding back, we hurt not only the team but also our teammates. Sometimes this is the only compelling argument that can convince a well-meaning teammate to step into the discomfort of telling someone what he or she needs to hear.

Holding Someone Accountable

Of the many benefits that coaching provides, a critical aspect is that of holding people accountable to their own goals and commitments. In fact, out of the following essential coaching dimensions, "Provides follow-up" routinely comes in last in terms of most leaders' focus and effectiveness. You can see the order below:

- Builds strong relationships.
- Facilitates action and results.
- Provides follow-up and accountability.

If you leave a coachee a "homework assignment"—some task or action they want to take and agree to complete before the next coaching conversation—make sure that you follow up. (These are actions that the employees have agreed to take, knowing the actions will help them move closer to their stated goals and desired future states.)

Remember the golden rule of management: "what gets measured gets completed." Your follow-up regarding coaching actions and commitments is just another way to "measure" progress.

1. Growth Mindset

Coaching is all about helping a person grow in their character and behavior, achieving greater results, and helping their organization move forward. So, both the coach and the coachee must have a growth mindset. The coach is looking for areas for growth that will be the most beneficial or areas that, if not addressed, will be detrimental. The coachee must have a positive mindset about growing and changing. The coaching process is about forward progress, which in essence is maturing and growing.

2. Break Old Patterns

For a leader or manager to become a coach, they must work hard at letting go of old patterns and past behaviors that they used in their position of authority. Behaviors such as advice-giving, command and control, or directing must be set aside or tempered. There are times when these are important, so one doesn't give them up completely. But from a coaching standpoint, you begin with understanding the big picture by asking questions, helping someone process their situation and take ownership. It is not a command and control or telling people, "These are the five things you must do and go do them." Those days of authoritarian leadership have passed and have proved to be very ineffective in today's fast-paced market and with emerging generations.

Chapter Three

THE COACHING CONVERSATION MADE PRACTICAL

There are two primary coaching conversations around which a coach must develop both a process and a skill set. The first conversation is known as the Level 10 Conversation (explained below). This helps coach and a potential coachee explore and brainstorm about where they are, where they would like to go, and what value that would be to each person. It is very open-ended and exploratory in nature. As a result of this conversation, both parties can begin to see and determine if coaching relationship would be beneficial for future growth.

The second conversation is the ongoing coaching conversation (also explained below). This is a five-step plan which helps one prepare, explore, apply, execute, and evaluate the results.

Level 10 Conversation

The Level 10 Conversation is all about exploring a person's dreams, desires, and needs at a deeper level in order to understand how coaching is going to make the most sense. The coach needs to begin to establish a relationship, but it's through curiosity and exploring they get to know the heart of the person. The potential coachee hopefully senses that the coach has a sincere desire to really know and help them move forward by the questions they're asking. This helps the relationship be both personal and substantive in order to solve needs and to make progress.

The following is a list of questions that successively move deeper in the process.

1. **Tell me about yourself, your business, your people.**
   - What is going on that is good?
   - If I could wave a realistic wand, where would you like to be in 6 months? (business, relationships, health, finances)
   - What is truly important to you?
   - What are your dreams and desires for the future?

Challenges—their impact and cost
   - What are your greatest and/or most urgent challenges?
   - To get a different result, what would have to change?
   - What prevents you from doing this?
   - What are the challenges costing you?

2. **Turn around—light at the end of the tunnel**
   - If you were to begin on the path to meet your dreams, what would that mean to you?
   - If you were able to address the challenges and begin to overcome them, what possibilities might this open to you?
   - What is the most important part of this conversation?

The Level 10 Conversation may also include what coaching is and that it includes:
   - Moving from chaos to clarity. Create clarity on your current starting point, urgent needs, and compelling desires.
   - Helping you develop a Personal Strategic Life Plan.
   - Identifying and upgrading your strengths and skills to help you increase your influence and impact.
   - Gaining mastery over limiting beliefs.
   - Solidifying a new framework on looking at and believing in yourself.
   - Optimizing your environment by reducing busyness in order to truly focus
   - Adding value to your life and your relationships.

In summary –
- The goal is to come alongside and help you become the best version of yourself that you could possibly be.
- The goal is to equip and inspire you to accomplish what you most desire.

The Coaching Conversation – A 5-Step Plan

This simple 5-step plan is aimed at determining the direction you wish to set for your coachee and creating a structure to guide you as you help them progress toward reaching their goal. This pattern can be used for your coaching conversations.

5-Step Plan

1. Preparation: Organize for the coaching meeting.
2. Exploration: Investigate and understand the issues and opportunities.
3. Application: Formulate a plan with goals and accountabilities.
4. Execution: Direct the coaching meeting, review progress, explore current issues, set next steps, schedule.
5. Direction: Keep committed to the big picture. Celebrate, alter actions as needed.

Preparation: Organize for coaching meetings

The coach needs to be present and ready to discuss with the coachee where they are and what is going on. It is good to review any notes from previous meetings and be prepared to follow up on any actions that they need to be held accountable for.

Exploration: Investigate and understand issues and opportunities.

The beginning of any coaching interaction needs to start with a clear purpose. The purpose tends to be one of three types of conversations: developmental (optimizing strengths), career (preparing for another role), or performance (overcoming obstacles or dealing with performance gaps).

To clarify this objective or purpose of the conversation, ask the coaching participant the following types of questions:

- What would you like to have accomplished at the end of this conversation?
- What does success look like when we are finished today?

This requires the coach to ask insightful questions, actively listen, be comfortable with silence, and see the situation through multiple perspectives. Have the coachee describe the current situation and clarify the primary objective for the conversation and the situation.

Application: Formulate a plan with goals and accountabilities

Goal setting is where the assessment and feedback turn into action to accomplish the purpose of the conversation. It is an important step in helping the coaching participant move forward and achieve a positive outcome. Guide the coaching participant to select a measurable goal that will stretch and challenge them.

- What are the three specific actions that will help you succeed?
- When will you accomplish these actions?
- How do these specific actions align with your overall performance targets?

This last step ensures accountability and provides encouragement to the coaching participant as they reach their goals. Unfortunately, this step is too often forgotten or not valued. Following up on the participant's agreed upon goals is critical in making sure actions happen. To this end, a great coach exhibits two skills: 1) recognizing progress and wins, and 2) encouraging the participant to manage through obstacles and secure the needed guidance to be successful.

- Who will support and celebrate with you in accomplishing your goals?
- What are possible obstacles that might prevent you from accomplishing them?

Execution: Direct the coaching meeting, review progress, explore current issues, set next steps, schedule.

A framework for a coaching session is to use the GROW model mentioned previously. (A full and comprehensive look at the GROW model will follows.) The setting of next steps and what they will be held accountable for is key for each meeting.

Direction: Keep committed to the big picture. Celebrate, alter actions as needed.

Celebrate! Congratulations, the coachee has reached their goal! Now is the time to reflect on the journey and celebrate the success. This is the time to ask, "What have you learned about yourself along the way?" "How did you reach your destination?" "What are you particularly proud of in terms of your accomplishment?" "How can you use the 'lessons learned' along the way to further your growth?"

The GROW Model

One of the best ways to get better at nondirective coaching is to try conversing using the GROW model, devised in the 1980s by Sir John Whitmore and others. GROW involves four action steps, the first letters of which give the model its name. It's easy to grasp conceptually, but it's harder to practice than you might imagine, because it requires training yourself to think in new ways about what your role and value are as a leader.

The GROW Model

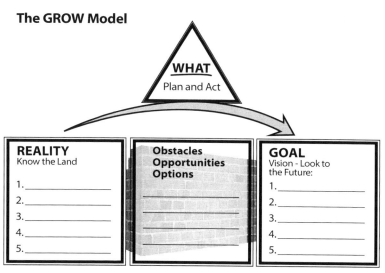

1. Establish the Goal

First, you and your team member need to look at the behavior that you want to change, and then structure this change as a goal that they want to achieve. Make sure that this is a SMART goal: one that is Specific, Measurable, Attainable, Relevant, Time-bound.

When doing this, it's useful to ask questions like:

- How will you know that you have achieved this goal or that the problem or issue is solved?
- Does this goal fit with the overall objectives? And does it fit with the team's objectives?

2. Examine the Current Reality

Next, describe your current reality. This is an important step. Too often, people try to solve a problem or reach a goal without fully considering the starting point, and often they're missing some information that they need in order to reach the goal effectively.

Useful coaching questions in this step include the following:

- What is happening now (what, who, when, and how often)? What is the effect or result of this?
- Have you already taken any steps towards your goal?
- Does this goal conflict with any other goals or objectives?

3. Explore the Obstacles, Opportunities, and Options

Examine the Obstacles and Opportunities that lie in front of you. Consider all the possible options for reaching the objective. Brainstorm as many good options as possible. Find Out More

- What else could you do? What if this or that constraint were removed? Would that change things?
- What are the advantages and disadvantages of each option?
- What factors or considerations will you use to weigh the options?
- What do you need to stop doing in order to achieve this goal?

4. What Will You Do

By examining the current reality and exploring the options, you will now have a good idea of how one can achieve this goal. The final step is to get to specific actions to move forward toward their goal. In doing this, you will help establish their will and boost the coachee's motivation.

- So, what will you do now, and when? What else will you do?
- What could stop you from moving forward? How will you overcome this?
- How can you keep yourself motivated? When do you need to review progress? Daily, weekly, monthly?

Finally, decide on a date when you'll both review the progress. This will provide some accountability and allow the coachee to change their approach if the original plan isn't working.

The following are coaching questions and a mindset going forward.

Issues. Why do you want coaching today?

Awareness. Get more info. Dig deep into past and current situations. How have you addressed this before? Tell me more.

Vision. If it were a 10, what would you like your world to look like? 30 days? 6 months? 1 year?

Strategy. What steps could you take in the next 30 days toward your vision? What resources and techniques can you use?

Goals. Get commitment level 1-10. What can you do between now and our next session to move this along?

Obstacles. What will hinder you from accomplishing these goals? (Internally and externally)

Coaches need to help the coachee set good goals which are known as SMART goals.

How to write SMART goals

S: Specific. In order for a goal to be effective, it needs to be specific. A specific goal answers questions like:

- What needs to be accomplished?
- Who's responsible for it?
- What steps need to be taken to achieve it?

M: Measurable. Specificity is a solid start, but quantifying your goals (that is, making sure they're measurable) makes it easier to track progress and know when you've reached the finish line.

A: Achievable. This is the point in the process when you give yourself a serious reality check. Goals should be realistic—*not* pedestals from which you inevitably tumble. Ask yourself: Is your objective something your team can reasonably accomplish? Safeguarding the achievability of your goal is much easier when you're the one setting it. However, that's not always the case. When goals are handed down from elsewhere, make sure to communicate any restraints you may be working under. Even if you can't shift the end goal, at least you can make your position (and any potential roadblocks) known up front,

R: Relevant. Here's where you need to think about the big picture. Why are you setting the goal that you're setting?

T: Time-bound. To properly measure success, you and your team need to be on the same page about when a goal has been reached. What's your time horizon? When will the team start creating and implementing the tasks they've identified? When will they finish?

SMART goals should have time-related parameters built in so everybody knows how to stay on track within a designated time frame. Knowing how to set goals using the SMART framework can help you succeed in setting and attaining goals, no matter how large or small.

	Objective	Example Questions
Grow	• Agree the discussion topic • Agree specific objectives for the session • Set a long-term goal or aim if this is appropriate	• What would you like to discuss? • What do you want to achieve in this session? • What differences would you like to see on leaving this session? • Do we have sufficient time available for you to attain this?

	Objective	Example Questions
Reality	• Invite self-assessment of topic & situation • Give specific examples of feedback • Check assumptions for validity • Discard Irrelevant assumptions & history	• How do you know that this is accurate? • How often does this occur? • What impact or effect does this have? • Are there other factors that are relevant? • What is X's perception of the situation? • What have you done or tried to date?
Obstacles	• Identify obstacles • Find out if the coachee believes there is more than one • You should consider & discuss the different types: people, resources, environment, etc.	• What prevents you from achieving your goal? • What else could be preventing you? • What personal changes do you think you would have to make to achieve your goal? • What is hindering you from changing? • Do any of your direct or indirect behaviors, attitudes, competencies, skills, etc. contribute to or help to maintain the situation?
Options	• Make sure to cover the full range of options • Invite suggestions from the coachee • Offer suggestions carefully • Ensure coachee makes the option choices	• What alternatives are there to that approach? • Who might be able to help you? • Would you like me to make suggestions? • Can you identify the pros and cons for that option? • Do you have a preferred option you'd like to act on?

	Objective	Example Questions
Way Forward	• Get a commitment to act • Identify the potential obstacles • Plan detailed actions within a set time frame • Agree what support will be given	• What are your next steps? • What time frame will you set? • Can you anticipate anything getting in your way? • How will you keep a log of your progress? • What support might you need? • How and when can you get that support?

Chapter Four

COACHING PROFESSIONALS

In the last chapter we talked about the coaching conversation that is generally the same conversation you have with each coachee when you meet with them. This conversation centers around the GROW model and the setting of SMART goals and holding the coachee accountable. In the next three chapters we are going to target three different audiences to which we apply the coaching conversation. First, we'll talk about coaching professionals and individuals where the focus is performance and growth—helping them to go deeper and broader on a personal basis. The primary goal is to become your very best.

Secondly, we will look at the area of coaching team leaders as those needs are different. The focus here is team leadership and leverage, specifically looking at process and production issues. The goal here is to help the team leader help their team and each individual grow.

Finally, we'll talk about coaching executive leaders who are at the highest level of a company and more strategically minded. The intention here is leadership development addressing effective influence and impact. The goal here is the develop your executive presence and leadership so you help grow future leaders.

Development Objectives

The following chart outlines specific development objectives for these three types of people being coached (professionals, team leaders, and executives) along with the five stages of leadership development which we will address in detail in a later chapter. The coaching of these three people groups is generally different in scope while using the same process of the GROW Model. We will look at each group and what is involved with each group.

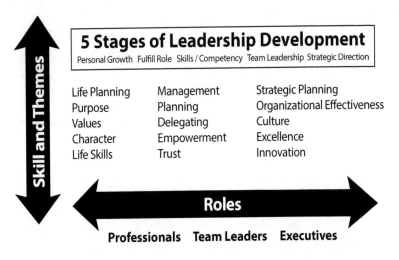

Coaching Professionals - The Core 4 Framework "Becoming Your Best"

Coaching Individuals and Professionals

The Core 4 Framework is a coaching structure that helps you as a leader to coach and develop every person to "becoming your best." The focus here is to grow your skills and give you tools to help you as a leader be able to coach professionals and individuals who work for you. The coachee will grow in depth and breath.

As a coaching leader you will model and demonstrate valuing each person wholly rather than simply focusing on the work performance and production. The framework considers both a person's life and their work and looks at the present and future elements of life. This breaks down into four quadrants:

Life / Present: Life Planning and Fulfillment

Work / Present: Work Performance and Results

Work / Future: Professional Development and Growth
Life / Future: Legacy Impact and Purpose

This Core 4 Framework becomes the basis for the four broad elements of how to coach an individual. Depending on the nature and focus of the coaching, any one of these elements might become the primary application. Ultimately, all four areas need to be addressed to complete the whole picture and perspective of an individual. We use this framework when we unpack the assessments, tools, and resources used in the coaching process.

Core 4 Framework

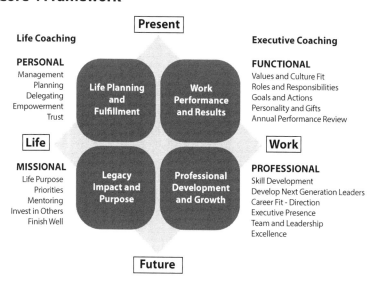

Let's walk through each of the four arenas to be coached. Life Coaching often begins with life in the present, whereas Executive Coaching would naturally focus on the work areas. Where you begin is based on the needs and desires of the person being coached. Life Coaching centers on two areas: personal and missional. Executive coaching centers on the two areas of functional and professional. We will break each of these four areas down.

Life Coaching

PERSONAL – Life Planning, Personal Values

Personal life coaching is focused on helping the individual be grounded and growing in maturity. It addresses the issues of personal values, values alignment, character, and developing trusting relationships. The following areas are the subject matter that every individual needs.

Values and Character

Marriage, Family

Life Planning

Relational Health

Community

Contentment

The goal for you as a coaching leader is to help the individual have a life plan that seeks to deliver mature growth, fulfillment, and satisfaction. The assessments tools and processes are outlined in Chapter 11. This first phase of the Core 4 process builds a foundation upon which an individual cannot only be their best but help others and the organization to do their best also. It is critical that this foundation is strong and secure. Care must be taken in terms of time to lay a strong foundational structure.

MISSIONAL – Purpose, Career Fit and Alignment

Once the personal foundation of life coaching has been established, the next critical step is defining the person's mission, which includes purpose, career fit, and alignment. This idea of purpose or "WHY" is at the heart of helping people be motivated and have a focus on their priorities and what's most important to them. It includes the following areas:

Life Purpose (A tool to develop your life purpose is in Chapter 11.)

Priorities

Mentoring

Invest in Others

Finish Well

The goal in this area of life coaching is for the individual to have a written life purpose but then cascades down into three-year targets, one-year goals, priorities, and then action steps. It allows them to not only know where they're going but how then to give their lives away through serving and mentoring as well as investing in the growth of others.

A secondary goal of the missional process is to help people who are in transition. This is either from one job to another or in ages and stages of life. It allows them to look at where they are what are their gifts and where do they want to go. It helps them address challenges and hurdles as well as to set priorities and goals for what they would like to see in the future.

The big idea is to finish well. It is to look back on your life and know that you've given your life to things of success, significance, and that have a lasting legacy.

The following tool is called the **One-Page Development Plan**, and it helps in both the personal and missional areas of life coaching. It is the final work product once one goes through the missional part of life coaching.

One-Page Development Plan

The One-Page Development Plan is just that—a one-page plan that helps you look at the big picture down to the details while keeping it to one page. This can be done for your individual life and your work and performance life. We highlight this planning tool here because it incorporates a Life Purpose along with Life Planning and Legacy Impact.

Purpose

ONE-PAGE STRATEGIC LIFE PLAN   Development Plan   **Goals: Keeping the End in Mind**   Know your "why," fulfillment, and make wise choices
Goal: Life Purpose Statement or your 3-word summary.   **What Difference Will It Make?**   **Values:**
Reality: Life Planning: How are you doing?   Where are your gaps?   See previous assessment—Acknowledge areas to be addressed.
Obstacles, Opportunities, Options: What are your obstacles, opportunities, and options? What are potential key actions you can take?   On your top 3 potential key target areas, do a SWOT analysis: Strengths, Weaknesses, Opportunities, Threats (helps in prioritizing).
What: Setting Priorities that Equal Outcome   Clear targets, goals, priorities, forward growth, and a life of excellence   Intimacy with Jesus, Marriage, Family and Children, Ministry, Finances, Work/Career, Business

3-Year Targets:	**1-Year Goals:**

What: Making the Most of Your Time.   Time management, accountability, and daily enjoyment. Accountability—Who?
Action Steps for 1-Year Goals: <u>**Ongoing Strategic Actions**</u>   **What Do I Need to Stop?**   **What Should I Start?**   **What Should I Continue?**
Resources Needed:
Who can help you? Who are you accountable to?

"Life is short – Make every day count." Faithful to opportunity. *"It is easy to make a fortune, it is very hard to make a difference."*

We all will give an account of how we spent our lives. The question is our faithfulness and commitment. We have a choice. A lack of purpose leads to: Frustration, Busyness, Discontentment, Regret. There is a significant and eternal cost to a lack of purpose. Purpose takes extreme ownership of the opportunities given us. The road map has four parts for living on purpose—excellence, character, stewardship, and others-centered. There is great reward when life is lived well, which includes:

Hope and Motivation	Joy and Contentment
Peace and Security	Significance and Satisfaction
Fruit and a Legacy/Impact	Reward and Recognition

1. **Purpose GIVES MEANING to our lives by connecting us to God's purposes.**
2. **Purpose helps us SET PRIORITIES to make wise decisions and overcome busyness.**
3. **Purpose generously ENGAGES our TIME, TALENT, and TREASURE to fulfill God's purposes.**
4. **Purpose CLARIFIES our HOPE so we can WALK BY FAITH in trials and triumphs.**

LIFE PURPOSE STATEMENT *"It is not about you." —Rick Warren*			
	Why is your life important? Two hundred years from now, what impact will your life make? What do you want to be remembered for? What difference will your life make?		
	Questions	**Reflections, Ideas, Thoughts, Heart**	**One Word**
Why	What are your life dreams and priorities that are beyond you? What lasting difference would you like to see in your life? What do you instinctively take action on? What frustrates you or causes you concern in this world?		
	Who do you serve? Who are you willing to sacrifice for?		
Who	Who do you do it for? Who are you helping improve or grow? Is it others-oriented?		
	What actions do you take? What are you good at that will help others?		
What	What do you live to do? What is the one thing you can truly teach someone else? What action is in your design? What makes you feel alive? What are your passions, gifts, strengths, and skills?		
	How do they change? How will this action make a difference?		
How	What do they want or need? How do they transform as a result of what you give them? What good works will it accomplish?		
Life Purpose Statement:			
3- to 4-Word Purpose:			

Purpose Example (Bruce Witt)

What	Who	Why	How
Equip	leaders	to leverage their gifts and passions	that multiply their influence and Kingdom impact.

Reflection: Work on your 3- to 4-Word Purpose

Application: Keep refining your purpose. With a written purpose, you can take steps to put your purpose into action.

Executive Coaching for Individuals and Professionals

Executive Coaching focuses both on work performance and professional growth development. It balances the functional in terms of executing the roles and responsibilities with the professional future growth of the individual.

FUNCTIONAL – Work Performance

The goal in coaching the Functional – Work Performance is to clarify the why, what, and how one is doing their agreed-upon responsibilities and goals. This is often used as a guide with a superior to assure there is complete alignment and that concrete steps of action are in place to accomplish the strategic goals. These tools and process are specifically geared to the current functioning in the job role and accomplishing set-out goals.

- Values and Culture Fit
- Clarify Roles and Responsibilities
- Goals and Action Steps
- Personality and Gifts
- Annual Performance Review

In Chapter 11 we provide various tools to help guide you as coach and coachee in the process of enhancing the work performance. These include the Five-Factor Assessment which helps assess the needs and priorities to help one achieve leadership growth, business results, leadership behaviors, team interactions, and company culture.

PROFESSIONAL – Growth and Professional Development
(Influence and Impact)

Coaching in the arena of the Professional – Growth and Professional Development shifts to the future needs and plans for the individual. It centers around the Professional Development Plan (PDP) and defining the necessary skills to accomplish your aspirations. This can be used for oneself and is very helpful in developing future leaders. One tool for development is the "Career Fit" which helps assure alignment long term. An excellence mindset is critical to this aspect of coaching.

- Professional Development Plan
- Skill Development
- Develop Next Generation Leaders
- Career Fit – Direction
- Executive Presence
- Team and Leadership – tools and framework on team leadership is found in the next chapter.
- Excellence Mindset – see Chapter 7

Chapter Five

COACHING LEADERS OF TEAMS — TEAM

To coach a leader in a team environment, you will need to encourage them to focus both on people (the team members) and the tasks (those things needed to be done to produce the desired results).

In terms of **people**, two important aspects to concentrate on are *trust*, which is about relationships and who people are, and *achieving*, which is how they will work together as a team. This work includes achieving synergy and good communication, which are the hallmarks of an environment or culture of helping one another.

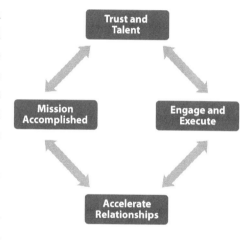

In terms of **tasks**, two crucial aspects are *execution*, which encompasses systems, processes, and getting the right things done with excellence, and *accomplishing the mission*, which achieves results that meet your goals and vision.

So, in the coaching process for each of these four areas, we will give the team leader some questions as well as several tools that will equip them to help their team members leverage their work and fulfill their responsibility.

TEAM

Trust and Talent – People and Growth
Engage and Execute – Strategy and Operations
Accelerate Relationships – Synergy and Teamwork
Mission Accomplished – Breakthroughs and Results

Trust and Talent

"The first job of any leader is to inspire trust. Trust affects speed and cost. When trust goes down speed goes down and costs go up. When trust goes up, speed will also go up and costs will go down."
— Stephen Covey

The first and foundational behavior of a cohesive team is trust. Although many people think of trust as the ability to predict a person's behavior based on past experience, that's not what we're talking about here. Rather in the context of a cohesive team trust means: *a willingness to be completely vulnerable with one another, to let down our guard admit our faults, and ask for help.*

Trust can only exist when we have confidence that our peers' intentions are good and that there's no reason to be protective or careful around the team.

Without it, the team members waste time and energy concealing their weaknesses and mistakes, hesitate to seek out help, and may assume the worst about their teammates' intentions and abilities. When there's trust on a team, we can take that energy required to manage our teammates' impressions of us and use it in more productive ways. We can draw on the collective skills and the support of the team to make our jobs easier, and we'll have a good foundation on which to build all other aspects of teamwork.

What does it look like to have trust on a team?
- Being unguarded and genuine with one another.
- Apologizing and being open about weaknesses and mistakes.
- Giving one another the benefit of the doubt rather than jumping to conclusions.

- Asking one another for help and input regarding areas of responsibility.

What makes it easier for you to build trust?

- Feeling like you won't be judged for expressing yourself.
- Working with people who are open and unguarded.
- Knowing your teammates are empathetic and accepting.
- Working in a social atmosphere where people take time to get to know one another.

Understanding the importance of trust, you can start looking at ways to build it on your team. This won't happen overnight. Building trust requires shared experiences over time, multiple instances of follow-through to develop credibility, and an in-depth understanding of the unique attributes of your colleagues. But working to develop the habits listed below can help accelerate the process with your teammates.

Develop good trust habits.

- Communicate, communicate, communicate! Work at communicating with your people about who they are, how they are doing, and what needs to be done.
- Create space for people to admit mistakes and weaknesses. Make sure you're leaving room in the conversation for more reserved teammates to open up.
- Asking leading but tactful questions can also help so as long as you don't push teammates to open up before they're ready. Also, make it a point to thank teammates who take a chance and are vulnerable with the group.

Don't take a teammate's reserve personally.

- Keep in mind that while many teammates may open up to your friendly approach, others may be more self-contained or solitary. Don't take the detachment personally.
- Recognize that everyone has different preferences and habits. Respect their inclination to work independently and move slowly when you see opportunities to establish a deeper connection.

Readily apologize for your mistakes.

- Owning up to and apologizing for mistakes doesn't diminish your value on the team. In fact, it can improve trust and communication between you and your teammates.
- Being open about your mistakes can encourage others to do the same.

Trust happens at three levels.

Building Personal Trust – Every individual must model and be committed to personal trust and being trustworthy. Here are specific actions that promote building personal trust.

- Exhibiting integrity, honesty, and faithfulness.
- Growing competency in skills
- Purposefully centering on others.

Growing Relational Trust – This level of trust is being built with others, which is at the heart of relationships. The following are actions that enhance relational trust.

- Being forthright and open
- Valuing and respecting others
- Seeking to understand
- Listening and being patient

Promoting Cultural Trust – This type of trust is centered around the team or organization as a whole. Organizational trust begins with a clarity and mutual commitment to the following questions.

- Who are we?
- Why do we exist?
- Where are we going?
- What are we doing ?
- Is "how" just as important as the results?

Coaching Questions

- How are you doing at being a person who is acting in trust?
- How is this team reflecting trust?
- Which actions of the team are most effective? Why?

- What actions, if modeled, would grow the trust in the team?

Engage and Execute

Execution is defined as performance, accomplishment, completing the task, finishing, doing the right things. Execution must be done with an "Excellence Mindset," modeling excellence, superiority, distinction, quality, being special, and having extraordinary behaviors.

Execute involves two primary focuses:

1. STRATEGY: CUSTOMER FIRST

The strategy must keep and *value customers* by focusing on a clear vision, a compelling plan, and engaged people.

"Real knowledge of the customer is absolutely essential. Without it, you cannot serve your market in a way that is superior to the competition." — **Horst Schulze**

Strategic Direction and Alignment – There are three aspects that make up having a clear Strategic Direction and Alignment. We just give you the overall picture here. More depth on what is involved can be found in the chapter eight where we present a big picture of having an "Excellent Mindset." (Other resources on this topic include *Good to Great* by Jim Collins and *Traction* by Gino Wickman.)

- Strategic Planning – Mission, Vision, Planning, Goal-setting
- Business Model Development – Sales and Marketing
- Customer Focused Execution

Coaching Questions

- How well are we serving our customers?
- What is the problem you are solving?
- How aligned are the strategies and goals?
- How aligned are the people with these strategic initiatives?

2. OPERATIONS: SUPERIOR PRODUCT

Operations must deliver a valuable product and service by continual improvement and effective simplicity.

"You need to find the root cause of any defect in order to eliminate it permanently. This is a vital part of continuous improvement in any organization. Each time you get to the bottom of a defect in this way, you improve your customer service while simultaneously lowering your cost over the long haul. It's a win-win all around."

— Horst Schulze

Operational Capacity and Delivery – here are three elements needed for building operations with the capacity to deliver a product or service of excellence.

- Excellence in Operations (continual improvement and change management)
- Superior Product Delivery (value added)
- Systems and Process (back office, efficiency, financial health)

Coaching Questions

- What is your primary product or service?
- How would you assess your current level of being superior?
- What are the critical factors or gaps that you must address?
- Who is responsible for this objective?
- What are the action plans that address it?
- What will it take to scale your operations?

Accelerate Relationships

The Accelerate Relationships component is characterized where people are valued, appreciated, and love to work together to accomplish great things. Leaders need to be highly selective in finding the best people. They do this by getting to know them and connect their strengths with the most suitable role. They invest in them with training and tools for success as well as empower them to take action. Building solid relationships is critical. Finally, leaders need to develop new leaders.

WORKFORCE: VALUED TEAM

"If you could get all the people in an organization rowing in the same direction, you could dominate any industry, in any market,

against any competition, at any time." — **Patrick Lencioni**

Teamwork Health and Leverage

- Clear Conflict Management Process
- Prioritization of processes that achieve objectives.
- Right People – Right Seats – Right Things

Every leader needs a team, and every team needs a leader. Leaders need to develop high-performance teams that model the relational competencies. This will include implementing a healthy process of goal-setting and follow-up while making sure the right people are in the right seats doing the right things. Team leaders must help others design, measure, and track goals. They develop a sense of care and commitment in the team. They also have a view of continual improvement and leading change. The following are three actions that team leaders do.

1. Cultivate Teamwork

- Connect people in teams to leverage their strengths.
- Develop a culture of intentionality, community, team, empowerment, and sacrifice.

2. Develop Your People by Investing and Training

- Take care of your people and they will never let you fail. Believe the best about people and they will exceed your expectations.
- Define Purpose - Give people a "why" and they will accomplish almost any "what" or "how."
- Provide people a purpose for work beyond a paycheck. This gives meaning, motivation, significance, and rewards.

3. Empower the People and Create Emerging Leaders

- Empowerment begins with specifying roles and responsibilities and providing the resources to accomplish them.
- Believe the best about people and give them the responsibility to do the work.
- Coach for excellence and empowerment.
- Grow your next generation of leadership.

Coaching Questions
- How is the health of your team?
- Are the team members aligned with their responsibilities and the goals?
- What are your processes for conflict resolution?
- How are you assuring that the right people are in the right seats doing the right things?
- What is your process to empower people to accomplish their tasks?
- How are you identifying emerging leaders and investing in them?

Mission Accomplished

Mission has a goal of accomplishing results by raising your bar of excellence in hitting your target.

Results Foundation

An Excellence Mindset will result in your organization greatly exceeding expectations and being successful. You and your organization will reflect success and leave a lasting impact by accomplishing your vision.

Results Exceptional Execution Practices

The following are three steps of application for a team leader.

1. **Foster Accountability – Accept no excuses.**
   - Be committed and intentional to go above and beyond.
   - Provide intentional accountability that helps each succeed while serving the customer well.

2. **Sustain your work and seek to scale it.**
   - Expand your Growth – Grow your excellence and people and opportunities will come to you.
   - Sustain the growth that you have accomplished. Don't be complacent, don't cut corners, seek efficiency not cost-cutting. Don't allow failure to block your learning and growing.
   - Scale the work by maintaining your core, benchmarking others, and taking calculated risks. Create the future by exploiting opportunities, not just by fixing problems.

3. **Celebrate your journey and destination.**
   - Enjoy the fruit of your labor.
   - Appreciate all of the people who worked for the success.
   - Envision what success may look like.

Results Actions and Application

- Action: Hold yourself accountable as well as others.
- Celebrate your victories.
- Persevere.
- Press into challenges.
- Keep looking up and looking beyond.

Coaching Questions

- What is your process of accountability?
- How are you assuring that the results are being accomplished?
- What are you doing to help celebrate wins and accomplishments?
- Are you growing in a position to be able to scale the business?

Chapter Six

COACHING LEADERSHIP EXECUTIVES – EXCEL

Coaching a leader at an executive level focuses primarily on Influence and Impact. Coaching an executive leader takes building on the coaching processes of a professional and a team leader. These capabilities need to be evident and growing as a foundation. We use the model known as EXCEL to coach executives to "fly higher" by focusing on five key ideas: strategy, developing future leaders, a thriving culture, excellence and effectiveness, and innovation in order to leverage and scale.

Strategic Planning Process – Leadership Revolution

The Framework

1. Company and Culture
2. Business Model
3. Critical Strategies
4. Organization/Teams
5. Comprehensive Plan
6. Committed Execution

Company and Culture – The focus and future of the company: They are the pillars that set the culture and behavior of the company.

a)   **Purpose – WHY?** Why do we exist? What good do we bring to the world? What is our just cause?

b)   **Mission – WHAT?** What is our primary activity? What do we do consistently?

c)   **Vision – WHERE?** Where are we going? What is the picture of success in 3-5 years? How would you describe it?

d)   **Values – HOW?** What are the core beliefs that will drive our company and hold us together? What is unique to how we do business? How are we using these values to help focus and make decisions?

e)   **Structure – WHO?** What is the current structure and organization? Who is the leadership? Are the roles clear?

f)   **Current Reality – NOW?** Where is the business now…financially? Business pipeline? What are the big issues?

Business Model

a)   **Economic Engine** – What business are you in? How do you make a profit?

b)   **Customers** – Who are your primary customers? 80/20 rule.

c)   **Key Products and Services** – What are your primary products and services that you deliver? Profitability?

d)   **Brand Promise** – What do you always deliver?

e)   **Point of View** – How do you stack up with competition? Points of parity? Points of differentiation?

f)   **Opportunities** – What are the opportunities both short-term and mid-term that could make a major difference in the trajectory of the business? What are the likelihood of these? What are the challenges? Brainstorm possibilities.

Critical Strategies

a)   **Key Result Areas – KRAs** – Key result areas are those areas where you need concrete progress, goals, and defined outcomes.

b)   **SWOT Analysis** – Strengths, Weaknesses, Opportunities,

Threats. This is a brainstorm of a SWOT process for each KRA.

c) **Key Strategies** – These are the strategies that come from the SWOT of "How" to accomplish the results and outcomes.

d) **Top Priorities** – The priorities help force-rank the strategies so there is a proper order and expenditure of resources.

Organization/Teams

a) **Leadership Team** – Oversight, Trust, Culture

b) **Teams/Teamwork** – Function, Division of labor. Right people / Right Seats. Competence, Strengths, Personality

Comprehensive Plan

a) **Goals** – These are 1-year SMART goals for departments, teams, and individuals. They are directed at achieving the strategies.

b) **Action Steps** – These are the monthly/quarterly actions to accomplish the goals. Include KPI's (Key Performance Indicators)

c) **One-Page Plan**

d) **The Excellence Factor Framework**

e) **Operations – Systems/Process** – The systems are in place (administration, technology, finances, HR, etc.). The processes of how work is completed are clear and accepted. Are your operations effective in delivering your product/service?

f) **Financial/Business Model** – The finance or business model works and is profitable. The finances are in place in terms of cash flow, capital investment, reserve fund, etc.

g) **Delivery** – The delivery of your product or service is functional and achieves a high level of excellence.

h) **Go to Market/Value Proposition** – There is a compelling marketing plan and way to compete well. The value proposition is defined and clear. How do we continue to add value?

i) **Alignment** – Once the plan and operations are developed, is there full alignment in terms of roles and responsibilities. ·

j) **Resources** – Do we need more people? Process? Technology? Capital?

k) **Accountability** – There is a defined and appropriate structure of accountability up and down with clear communication.

Committed Execution

a) **Cycle of Success** – Annual, Quarterly, Monthly, Weekly meeting process.

b) **Communication** – There is both a process and execution of communication up and down and within the teams that challenges, and opportunities are surfaced, discussed, and resolved.

c) **The Excellence Factor Framework** – This a five-fold process that focuses and executes with the highest level of excellence. Trusted Culture, Customer First, Superior Product, Valued Team, Raving Fans

d) **Innovation/Change** – There is an entrepreneurial mindset that seeks to innovate and change when needed.

e) **Meeting Cadence** – There is clarity on timing and process for meetings at all levels to ensure they are functional and not burdensome.

The Process – 6 Steps of the Visioning Planning Process

Step 1: Gather the Team

- Get the right people at the leadership level on the bus (they are your most important asset).
- Engage in the process.

Step 2: Look to the Future

- Know you purpose. Ask and answer – Why? Why is it important? (What is the good you are seeking and the problem you are solving). Why now? Why us?
- Create a sense of Urgency.

Step 3: Seek a Clear Vision

- Seek a clear picture of your vision. Where?
- Define values/mission (values + behavior = culture).
- Gain input and counsel.
- Picture of Success

Step 4: Know the Land
- Understand your context, who are you serving? What do they need or want?
- Know your strengths and weaknesses.
- Be honest about your capacity.
- See the opportunities and barriers.

Step 5: Plan and Act – Strategy and Goal Setting
- Define your KRA's – key result areas.
- Plan and prioritize strategic steps and goals.
- Establish KPI's – key performance indicators.
- Empower people for action and teamwork with clear roles and responsibilities. Right people in right seats.

Step 6: Check yourself
- Examine yourself – Are you on track? How do you measure and hold yourself accountable?
- Seek excellence, improvement, and innovation.

One Page Strategic Plan

Purpose		
Mission		
Vision		
Values		
Goals		

	Growth			Enabling		
Core Strategies						
KPI						
Strategic Initiatives						
Steward						

EXCEL

E – Execute the Strategic Plan

X – Multiplying Leaders

C – Cultural Focus

E – Excellence and Effectiveness

L – Leverage Innovation for Scale

E – Execute the Strategic Plan

Executives are in roles and responsibilities where results and delivering on the strategic plan are what is absolutely expected of them. Thus, the coaching needs to be along the lines of understanding and communicating the strategic plan to their leadership teams and, in turn, helping their teams accomplish their goals and objectives. A critical component of this process is assuring alignment with the particular teams and verifying their commitment to the plan and process.

Coaching the executive could also include a number of the items previously detailed in the section on Professionals – Growth and Development, in particular on gaining the needed skills that the executive might need. It would be advisable to craft a PDP (Professional Development Plan) for the executive.

In some cases, you may have to help the executive develop the strategic plan, which would include the mission and vision for the organization or team. This vision needs to be clear, concise, comprehensive, and compelling.

X – Multiplying Leaders

The second absolute is for executives to grow their direct reports in their leadership as well as to grow future leaders for the long term. This is where The Coaching Leader is so valuable in helping the executive grow and develop their team.

We will devote an in-depth focus on Leadership Development in Chapter 10. We review the 5 Stages of Leadership Development along with key tools, processes, skills, and resources for each.

C – Cultural Focus

The third element that is imperative for an executive to master is the oversight and execution of the culture of their team or organization. This culture focus includes defining and modeling the core values as well as setting the relational environment that values people and customers alike. Culture ultimately will be more important than plan, because plans change and evolve while the culture needs to be stable and healthy.

E – Excellence and Effectiveness

Executive leaders need to cast and deliver on excellence and effectiveness in everything they do. This applies to all areas of skill development and the system /process development and improvement. In Chapter 7 we will unpack a thorough perspective of what excellence delivery looks like, also known as "The Excellence Factor." Effectiveness has a goal of accomplishment within healthy relationships.

L – Leverage Innovation for Scale

The final key for executive is growing or scaling the business. Most organizations are not satisfied with the status quo, so how to build the organization in terms of results, processes, and people is foundational. This growth and scale will take innovation and thinking outside the box to create change. A number of related topics that will help an executive scale the business are covered in Chapter 12 and include Handling Challenges and Conflict, Leading Change, and Situational Leadership – Lead According to Need.

Coaching executives requires a bifocal vision: managing the current challenges and problems of the business while keeping an eye to the horizon and how to accomplish the vision and strategic plan, most likely 3-5 years out.

Chapter Seven

COACHING FOR AN EXCELLENCE MINDSET – THE EXCELLENCE FACTOR

We need to coach people to think and act with an attitude of excellence, which will bring extraordinary results. To achieve results with excellence, one needs to understand both the problems and opportunities that lie ahead. The following lists detail these issues.

The Top Problems in Today's Market – 3 Global IBM Studies

- Uncertainty, Disruptive Markets, and Forces
- Increasing Competition (foreign, Internet)
- Pace, Complexity, and Volume of Information
- Recruit, Keep, and Motivate Quality Talent
- How to be Flexible, Change, and Scale
- Finding and Retaining Profitable Customers
- Cash Flow Issues and Too Much Overhead

Addressing the major opportunities of your organization.

- Leadership Presence – provides oversight, motivation, and culture.
- Strategic Direction – overcomes uncertainty and busyness to compete in a global economy.
- Productivity and Growth – increasing sales growth and profitability through new products, markets, and customers.
- People Challenges – retaining talent, working remotely, and team dynamics.

- Executing the Priorities – getting the right things done that ensure you outclass your competition.

To meet the problems of the day and the future opportunities, a pursuit of excellence is both critical and the best strategy going forward. "The Excellence Factor" is a model that will help those who you coach and those leaders who incorporate the skills of coaching to be very effective.

The Excellence Factor unpacks a framework of five catalytic leadership disciplines that have an explosive growth through focus on, commitment to, and delivery of excellence.

Leadership establishes a **Trust Culture** as the foundation for a *Compelling Direction.*

Strategy prioritizes a **Customer First** mindset that produces a *Focused Alignment.*

Operations deliver a **Superior Product** through *Exceptional Execution.*

Workforce leverages talent as a **Valued Team** with an *Empowered Engagement.*

Results are produced by **Raving Fans** allowing for *Scalable Growth.*

The Excellence Factor Framework

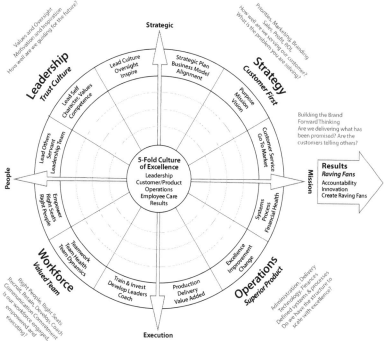

The Excellence Factor Model – 5-Fold Culture of Excellence is at the heart of a transformative culture and vibrant organization.

The following is more detailed information on these five excellence factors. These will help frame the picture and specifics involved. Coaching questions can be formed from this perspective.

- **LEADERSHIP: TRUST CULTURE** – *"The first job of any leader is to inspire trust. Trust affects speed and cost. When trust goes down speed goes down and costs go up. When trust goes up, speed will also go up and costs will go down."* — **Stephen Covey**

  Leadership is Trusted. Leaders serve and guide a culture of trust with a character of humility and integrity. Provide oversight and inspiration. Utilize the collective IQ of a leadership team with the right people in the right seats.

- ***STRATEGY: CUSTOMER FIRST*** – *"Real knowledge of the customer is absolutely essential. Without it, you cannot serve your market in a way that is superior to the competition."* — **Horst Schulze**

  Strategy Prioritizes Valuing your Customer. Knowledge of the customer's needs and desires is the foundation to valuing them. Give the customer excellence in service. Appreciate the customer with recognition and personalized service.

- ***OPERATIONS: SUPERIOR PRODUCT*** – *"You need to find the root cause of any defect in order to eliminate it permanently. This is a vital part of continuous improvement in any organization. Each time you get to the bottom of a defect in this way, you improve your customer service while simultaneously lowering your cost over the long haul. It's a win-win all around."* — **Horst Schulze**

  Operations Deliver an Exceptional Product / Service. Performance is the key to excelling in achieving goals. Operations execute to produce profitability and productivity as results. Excellence provides the very best product or service with a view of continual improvement.

- ***WORKFORCE: VALUED TEAM*** – *"If you could get all the people in an organization rowing in the same direction, you could dominate any industry, in any market, against any competition, at any time."* — **Patrick Lencioni**

  The workforce is Valued, Empowered, and Works as a Team. Appreciation provides recognition and thanks for the contributions of others. Empowerment and alignment come when the objectives and its employees are on the same page. Teamwork encompasses collaboration, communication, and respect between team members.

- ***RESULTS: RAVING FANS*** – *"The difference is that raving fans, unlike satisfied customers, become part of your sales forces. They tell friends, family, and co-workers about your services and your products. And, of course, good things will happen."* — **Mac Anderson**

  Results that are Strategic, Sustainable, and Scalable. There is accountability, innovation, and a continual look to the future. Aware of their marketplace, competition, and possible need to reinvent themselves.

The assessment that follows on the next three pages helps you (the coach) and the executive being coached (the coachee) have a clear way of defining strengths, weaknesses, and gaps to address.

The Excellence Factor Assessment

(Rate each of the 40 factors on a scale of 1-5, with 5 as excellent.)

LEADERSHIP	Champion a Trust Culture of Excellence
STRATEGY	Focus on Customer First Strategic Planning
OPERATIONS	Work on the Business to Deliver a Superior Product
WORKFORCE	Valued Team that is Empowered
RESULTS	Raving Fans allowing Scalable Growth

LEADERSHIP   **Subtotal:** _____

1. Leadership Team – defined with who & how they function _____
2. Board of Directors or equivalent – who, type, oversight _____
3. Culture – a compelling place of value & trust, mindset of excellence, clear values _____
4. Lead Self – person of trust, character, maturity _____
5. Servant Heart – value and care for people _____
6. Develops the Next Leaders – mentor, coach, succession _____
7. Exercises Oversight Responsibility – clear priorities, executes, set the values _____
8. Right people are in the right seats on leadership team _____

STRATEGY   **Subtotal:** _____

1. Defined Mission and Vision _____
2. Developed Comprehensive Plan – set clear long-term objectives (3-5 yr.) / KPI's _____
3. Identifiable Goals and Action Steps (1 yr. – 6 mo.) _____
4. Alignment with People – committed, buy-in _____
5. Economic Engine – business model is clear _____
6. Customer First Focus – passion of serving and providing excellence _____
7. Product/Service of Excellence _____
8. Strategy has contingencies for unplanned challenges _____

OPERATIONS   Subtotal: _____

1. Infrastructure/organization – clear & simple; administration, finances, etc.   _____
2. Resources – have acquired needed finances and funding   _____
3. Technology – systems, track data is in place and functional   _____
4. Communication – internal/external is clear and effective, meetings work   _____
5. Teach/training processes for growth   _____
6. Excellence and continual improvement process are embraced   _____
7. Delivery – go to market is working   _____
8. Financial operations are in place and have accountability   _____

WORKFORCE   Subtotal: _____

1. Function in teams and teamwork   _____
2. Engagement of employees – personality and strengths known, empowered   _____
3. Roles and responsibility clear – right people/right seats   _____
4. Performance review process for all   _____
5. Conflict resolution process   _____
6. Training and investment to grow, teach an excellent mindset   _____
7. Scorecard – clear and usable, not too complicated   _____
8. A dedicated team can go into action when needed   _____

RESULTS   Subtotal: _____

1. Reporting and feedback – up and down the organization   _____
2. Accountability – individually and collectively is functional   _____
3. Sustainability of the business is certain, scalability is being pursued   _____
4. Mindset of excellence is celebrated and continuing   _____
5. Innovation and change management   _____
6. Celebrate wins and individual performance   _____
7. Legacy impact – affect beyond the organization   _____
8. Processes are in place for innovation and reinventing the business   _____

Total the 5 disciplines & multiply by .5 for a score based on 100 being perfect.

The Excellence Factor Score: _____ **x .5 =** _____

List Notable Gaps / Highest Priorities / Actions Steps:

The Excellence Factor Checklist – 20 Critical Factors

These 20 critical factors form a checklist of factors to understand where you are and where you need to grow. This is just one more way to ask key questions in the coaching process.

Leadership

1. *LEADERS LEADING*

   Do you have leaders in the organization, not managers, inspiring employees with motivation and purpose?

2. *ORGANIZATIONAL CULTURE*

   Do leaders and employees have rapport, connection, and a culture of trust? How are they at representing the values?

3. *DEVELOPING LEADERS*

   Are leaders growing in personal and professional confidence to make strong decisions for the organization?

Strategy

1. **VISION MATTERS**

   Do you have a compelling destination in mind for your company? Is it good for all involved?

2. **KNOW YOUR CUSTOMER**

   Do you know your customer, their needs and wants? Do you use surveys? When sentiments are discovered, do you adapt?

3. **TIE IT TOGETHER**

   Have you developed a cohesive strategy from customer experience, employee care, and product and service user experience that expresses one cohesive brand?

4. **SUPREME OBJECTIVES**

   Can your employees recite your three or four most important business objectives?

Operations

1. **SERVICE PROCESS**

   Do you have a replicable process that serves as the standard for your employees?

2. **HANDLING COMPLAINTS**

   Are your employees trained and equipped to handle simple and complex complaints from customers?

3. **SYSTEMS OF REPETITION**

   Have you created systems that cause important values and behaviors to be repeated daily?

4. **DELIVERY**

   What are you doing to maintain defect-free delivery that is also timely and friendly?

5. **IMPROVEMENT**

   What are you doing to continually improve your product/service?

6. **PRODUCT/SERVICE OF EXCELLENCE**

   What are you doing to have a product or service of excellence?

Workforce

1. **PEOPLE SELECTION**

   Do you have the right people selected for your roles? Have you offered them inspiring purpose?

2. **CUSTOMER TYPES**

   Does your team understand the important differences between satisfied, dissatisfied, and loyal customers?

3. **ORIENTATION/ONBOARDING**

   Do your onboarding, orientation, and training processes communicate your company purpose before job functions?

4. **TEAMWORK**

   Are the people working in effective team environments that are cohesive and empowered?

Results

1. **PICKING THE RIGHT METRICS**

   Does your team have a firm grasp on the most helpful metrics to measure progress and success?

   Is your team capturing the right data to produce the insights?

2. **CELEBRATE**

   What are you doing to celebrate personal and corporate wins?

3. **INNOVATION**

   How are you innovating to stay ahead of the competition? What are you doing to benchmark yourself?

Chapter Eight

COACHING TO SOLVE A PROBLEM

Below the Surface – What will sink your ship?

The following framework is a way of trying to find the heart of a problem area between people or teams. The "Below the Surface" framework helps you identify issues and problems of people and business growth by starting broad and then drilling down from Purpose to Process to People. It is important to start higher because you could solve certain issues on a personal level and still have issues of process or purpose. Yet if you address the Purpose or Process challenges it can clear up personal issues.

As a coach, you begin to dig into understanding what is below the surface by asking questions related to the bullet points below. Just keep working your way down the list.

A coach assesses problems and challenges in three broad areas: purpose, process, and people. Within each of these areas there are key questions and specific issues that need to be addressed. The following outlines how to approach and assess when problems arise.

Purpose – Why? – Big Picture
1. **Mission, Vision, Plan** – Clarity & Strategic Planning
   Lack of clarity (understanding, commitment, vision casting)
   Uncertainty, lack of alignment and motivation, SWOT analysis
2. **Culture** – Connected & Loyalty
   Trust issues, unclear or undefined values, factions

Process – What/How? – Smart

3. **Roles and Goals** – Focus & Direction
   Job expectations not clear – defined responsibilities, personal planning
   Need coaching and development, performance improvement, accountability

4. **The Bus** – Right People, Right Seats, Right Things – Priorities & Retention
   People selection, need assessment, delegation
   Personal planning and goal setting

5. **Competence** – Skills, Talent, & Growth
   Need for training, gap assessment, personal SWOT

People – Who? – Healthy

6. **Relationships** – Teams and Interpersonal Harmony & Support
   Communication challenges, personality differences, team dynamics mixed, people feel cared for.
   5 Behaviors, conflict resolution
   Clearing conversation

7. **Internal** – Personal Issues – Whole & Strong
   Counseling, growth and development, maturity

Five Business Conditions and Challenges

Macro-scale issues that organizations or teams face revolve around these Five Business Conditions and Challenges. Again, as a coach these form a way to think through and identify the problem areas on a larger scale.

1. **Leadership and Culture**
2. **Organizational Strategy and Alignment**
3. **Operating Discipline and Value Creation**
4. **Teamwork and Emotional Endurance**
5. **Predictability of Performance and Results**

The Leadership and Culture condition addresses the question, "How well are the leaders guiding and serving to yield a vibrant culture?" Leaders build a culture of trust, commitment, and growth by guiding and serving.

The Organizational Strategy and Alignment condition addresses the question, "Is the business growth-capable?" Alignment is most strongly related to performance suggesting the elements the condition measures are a critical foundation for growth. Alignment comes with a clear strategic plan that includes the mission, vision, and plan.

The Operating Discipline and Value Creation condition addresses the question, "Can the business scale in delivering excellence to the customer?" The key is growing excellence at all levels that brings value to the customer. It looks at businesses' efforts to identify and track key performance indicators and build a capacity for continual improvement.

The Teamwork and Emotional Endurance condition addresses the question, "Can employees and other stakeholders work well together and maintain emotional health to endure the growth journey?" It looks at businesses' efforts to monitor and maintain an emotional commitment that helps retain talent.

The Predictability of Performance and Results condition addresses the question, "Are the decision-makers continuously hitting their targets, growing, and innovating?" It recognizes that leaders can learn from past growth experiences to improve their decision-making and leadership.

Five Helpful Questions

The following five questions are very helpful for leaders to ask of their teams, employees, and customers. The answers will help them gain much needed information and things that will help the leader and the team set clear priorities as well as stop doing certain things.

1. What are the Top Three Things that are STRENGTHS (right things, already effective) with the services and support of _____ that we should CONTINUE?

2. What are the Top Three Things that are WEAKNESSES (deficient) with the services and support of _____ that we should IMPROVE?

3. What are the Top Three Things that are UNPRODUCTIVE (time wasters – busyness) with the services and support of _____ that we should STOP?

4. What are the Top Three Things that are CONFUSING (threats) about the services and support of _____ that we should CLARIFY?

5. What are the Top Three Things that are MISSING (opportunities and potentials) in the services and support of _____ that we should CREATE?

Consider asking the preceding questions on Three Levels

1. **Personal** – leader as coach, think entrepreneurial, increasing your strategic mindset

2. **Internal** – enhance execution, make more efficient, better communication, team development, leadership development

3. **External** – (interacting with Sales, HR, Leadership, etc.) Their input on Continue? Improve? Stop? Clarify? Create?

Chapter Nine

COACHING AND LEADERSHIP DEVELOPMENT

In this chapter on Coaching and Leadership Development we are going to look at three different ways or frameworks that help you understand leadership development. The first model is the 5 Stages of Leadership Development which begins with the inside and then works outward.

The second model is one that was developed by John Maxwell which talks about the Five Levels of Leadership, it is similar, but different, and just another way to look at leadership development.

A third model is that of Jim Collins in *Good to Great*, where he has again 5 levels of leadership. We review all of these models to give you more than one way to look at the developing of yourself as a leader as well as coaching others to be leaders. There is a chart that compares and contrasts similarities and differences on this leadership development continuum. The goal is to broaden your approach as you coach leadership development and to help you grow as a leader yourself.

Because we are all leaders, we should have the perspective of growing and developing our leadership perspective, skills, and capacity. The three tracks of leadership development combine the ideas from John Maxwell's "5 Levels of Leadership" along with Jim Collin's "Level 5 Leadership." We then look at the skills involved in developing leaders at each of these 5 levels. This becomes a framework for leaders to assess themselves as well as develop their professional development plan along the lines of where they are and where they want to grow to. This plan helps them identify certain skills that it takes to become a leader at a higher level. Coaching is just one element, yet it is a significant element in terms of growth.

True leadership isn't about having a certain job, title, or position. True leadership is about investing in people, building relationships, and inspiring them. True leadership is about achieving results and building a team—a team that produces. True leadership is about helping people develop their skills to become leaders themselves. True leaders who have skill and dedication can reach the pinnacle of leadership—extending their influence for the benefit of others, creating true leaders following behind.

Growing a Leadership Development Culture

Assessment

1. Do we agree on a clear picture of leadership and the development process? **Define it.** (Agree and develop)

2. Do the current and emerging leaders have the skills to lead well? **Teach it.** (Training)

    What are the essential skills? What do we do?

    What is your process of training?

3. Do your emerging leaders have ample opportunities to lead? **Practice it.** (Tasks risk, give opportunities)

    Do we identify the skills, problems, challenges, opportunities you want them to have?

    Do we give them opportunities?

4. Do you have an objective way to measure leadership effectiveness? **Measure it.** (Have a score card)

    Do you have a series of metrics that measure? (performance, readiness, character)

    Are you loose, dynamic, and flexible?

5. Do your current leaders model the desired behaviors for your organization? **Model it.** (Put it into action)

    How are leaders modeling their leadership?

    Are they servant leaders?

So these are Commitments of a leadership culture: **Define it, Teach it, Practice it, Measure it, Model it.** How are we responding?

Leadership Development Process for Organizations

The Leadership Development Process for an Organization comprises four primary areas: the Leadership Framework, the Leadership Pipeline, the Leadership SERVE BIG Model, and Leadership Excellence Best Practices.

The Leadership Framework looks at the three big buckets that frame the function of leadership: culture, work performance, and leadership development and growth. Leaders need to function in all three areas and be proficient at helping others grow in these areas.

The Leadership Pipeline outlines the 5 Levels of Leadership with the key characteristics, what does competency look like, and what are the skills needed at each level. The focus here is to identify and assess where your leaders are and determine a growth process for them to achieve their highest potential. Not everyone will be a leader of leaders or an organizational leader.

The Leadership SERVE BIG Model helps give the heart and actions for growing as a leader. This helps a leader know their areas of strength and areas of growth.

The Leadership Excellence – Best Practices is a structure of the actions and big picture of the responsibilities of leadership and being a servant leader. The Leadership Excellence Best Practices frames the structure, the functions, and the execution of leadership.

Leadership Framework

The Big Buckets	Culture	Work Performance	Leadership Development and Growth
Key Components	Trust Belief in Others Mission Vision Values Alignment	1. Personal Attitude and Growth mindset 2. Roles/Responsibilities – Clarity 3. Goals Quarterly Targets 4. Action Steps Team – Goals Communication/Alignment	Leadership Skill Development Delegation Empowerment Planning Time Management Communication Team Leadership Coaching _____ _____
Goals	Unity in Heart and Culture Personal and Team Growth Multiplying Results	Personality Profile Purpose Goals and work growth plan Annual Performance Review	PDP – Professional Development Plan Mentoring
Process	Culture Alignment Commitment	Direct Reporting Coaching Training Process	Initiated at Direct Level Self-Directed/Mentor
Needs	Heart	Excellence	Extreme Ownership Future Dreams and Direction
Tools and Resources	Monthly Leadership Meetings Growth through Retreats	Personality Profile Purpose Goals and work growth plan Annual Performance Review	PDP – Professional Development Plan Mentoring

Leadership Pipeline
Developing Leaders to their Highest Potential

Lead Self – Intimacy that brings about self-awareness and alignment to values – Foundation

This is a view of leadership that sets character (humility and integrity) and personal values as the foundation and functions with a priority of serving others. Leaders recognize their role of guiding and being responsible to establish a healthy culture. They are proactive in having a personal development plan for healthy growth. Self-awareness includes knowing their personality is grounded in the character of humility, integrity, and trustworthiness.

- Sense of humility, integrity, and teachability.
- Attitude – thankful, hope, purpose, resilience in chaos. Stewardship – time, talent, treasure, truth, relationships, grace.
- Commits to self-awareness, builds character, demonstrates integrity.
- Discover Your Leadership Personality.
- Authentic Leadership, being vulnerable.
- Building a Personal Development Plan.

Lead People – People and Relationships

Leading others focuses on valuing others, developing others, and establishing healthy, trusting relationships with the people you work with. Leaders need the strengths and talents of others, so relationships are directly tied to effectiveness and resolving conflicts. Leaders will learn about Situational Leadership (leading according to the needs of the team) and will gain the skills of coaching as a process for developing people and leaders.

- Building trust and a care for others .
- Body – gifts, need one another.
- Balancing people and mission.
- Values others and has healthy relationships, develops trust.
- Conflict resolution, Critical Conversations or The Clearing Model.

Lead Teams – Developing Effective Teams

Every leader needs a team and every team needs a leader. Leaders will be developed in leading high-performance teams building on the relational competencies gained in previous sessions. This will include implementing a healthy process of goal-setting and follow-up while making sure the right people and in the right seats doing the right things.

- Be a Team Player. Builds high-performing teams.
- Building Cohesive Teams / 5 Dysfunctions.
- Living and Leading through Change.

Lead Leaders – Developing the Next Generation of Leaders

Leaders will learn how to coach and develop leaders. They also know, model, and teach Situational Leadership (leading according to the needs of the team) and will gain the skills of coaching as a process for developing people and leaders.

- Focuses on developing others.
- Coaching and developing leaders.
- Leadership and Management Practices.
- Situational Leadership and the Leader as a Coach.

Lead Organizations – Lead the Culture. Growing Results

Leaders will bring all these skills and processes together to increase engagement and produce growing results. They will gain a perspective on the need for innovation and the commitment to excellence to balance the current work with future direction. Guide Skillfully, Strategic Acumen (Skill Development), and Skillful leadership are critical to the health and growth of the leader, their team, and the organization. The best leaders are continually learning and practicing proficiency. Communication skills are foundational to effectiveness. Other skills that will be covered are planning, delegating, feedback, and decision-making.

- Servant Leadership.
- Eternal in the temporal, make a difference.
- Grows a culture of valuing people and results.
- Strategic Planning, concentrates on delivering results.

- Models and encourages strategic, critical thinking.
- Grows Skills: delegate, empower, oversight, communication, time management.

Leadership SERVE BIG Model – Level Up your Leadership for Radical Impact

5 Core Disciplines

S	Shape your Leadership to build a Trust Culture	*Champion the Values*
E	Engage with Vision and Strategy with an Others-first Focus	*Clarify your Future*
R	Refine your Process and Operations to deliver a Superior Product	*Excellence Continuously*
V	Value Teams and Teamwork	*Empower and Develop Others*
E	Excel at Results creating a Movement	*Results through Relationships*

3 Key Accelerators

B	Be a Coach to Grow and Multiply Talent	Multiply your Leadership Bench
I	Improve your Use of Time for greater Effectiveness	Right Priorities Lead to Better Outcomes
G	Grow through Change	Innovation leads to Transformation

Shape your Leadership to build a Trust Culture – WHO?

Values are the foundation of our calling to leadership.

- Lead Self – be a servant – Character (Being) – Humility, Integrity, Trustworthy. Build skills, model the values.
- Lead Others – give oversight and vision, invest and build the next generation of leaders.
- Lead the Culture – Build trust, exercise care, consistency, inspiration – take extreme ownership.

Engage with Vision and Strategy with an Others-first Focus – WHY?

Our vision is to make a difference in lives. We have clarity of purpose and aligned the organizational purpose.

- Bring clarity of purpose, vision, and mission. Communicate a compelling vision to attract and engage others.

- <u>Plan strategically</u> with a larger plan, goals, and actions to create alignment.
- <u>Keep focused on your customer</u> – who you are serving and how you put them first and meet their needs. Pursue excellence.

Refine Process and Operations to deliver a Superior Product – HOW?

Do all things with Excellence – Good for all, positive influence, draws people to you. Do things with all your heart.

- Be operationally sound. Set your systems and processes to increase your impact. Balance structure with adaptability.
- Seek Excellence – Improve continuously. Instill it with everyone.
- Deliver a superior product/service. Execute on your brand promise.

Value Teams and Teamwork – WITH?

Two are better than one. The whole is greater than the one – collective IQ, gifts of the team. Value people.

- <u>Work together</u> to leverage the wisdom and giftedness of the team. Have clarity of aligned roles and goals.
- <u>Invest, build, and train</u> the members of the team. Build and develop the next generation of leaders. Be a coach.
- <u>Empower and delegate</u> to others – Recruit and select the right people, placed in right seats, for the right job.

Excel at Results Creating a Movement – WHAT?

Be faithful in the process – it will produce the outcome. Focus on relationships more than size, numbers, or money.

- <u>Be accountable</u> to yourself, to your people, and to the process. Value results and relationships. Stewardship.
- <u>Be innovative</u> and willing to change. Be aware of disruptions and be a disrupter. Keep agile.
- <u>Keep a growth mindset.</u> Sustain and scale according to your plan. Work on the business. Get outside counsel.

Be a Coach to Grow and Multiply Talent – WHERE?

Multiply your Leadership Bench – the skills of coaching will greatly increase your influence.

- <u>Gain the skills of coaching:</u> Listen, ask, empower. It is simple and is the essence of empowering and delegating.
- <u>Apply coaching to retain and grow talent.</u> People are your great asset.
- <u>Grow your influence with coaching.</u> Coaching is highly effective with the next generations.

Improve Your Use of Time for Greater Effectiveness – WHEN?

Right Priorities Lead to Better Outcomes – focus on priorities not just goals.

- <u>Stop before you start</u> to create margin and take on the right priorities.
- <u>Priorities equal outcome.</u> Not everything that is urgent is important.
- <u>Less is more.</u> One needs to be refreshed and recharged to be better.

Grow through Change – NEXT?

Innovation leads to Transformation – everything is continually changing, be ready to wisely change.

- Excellence is everything. Change for excellence and the world will come to you.
- Change is a process. It takes motivation, vision, planning, trust.
- Change must be strategic. Don't change for the sake of change. Focus on the 80/20.

Leadership Excellence Best Practices

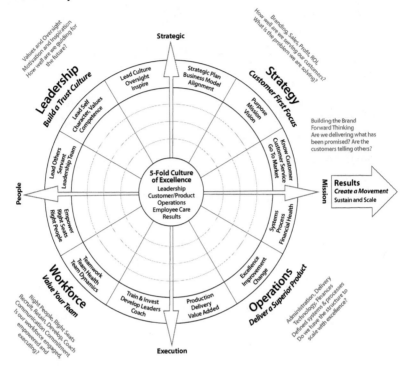

In this section we will look at two more models for leadership development. The first is from John Maxwell and the second is from Jim Collins. The goal here is to expose you to three models of development and then adapt them to your unique context.

5 Levels of Leadership – John Maxwell

The overview of John C. Maxwell's 5 Levels of Leadership:

1. Position – People follow because they have to.
2. Permission – People follow because they want to.
3. Production – People follow because of what you have done for the organization.
4. People Development – People follow because of what you have done for them.

5. Pinnacle – People follow because of who you are and what you represent.

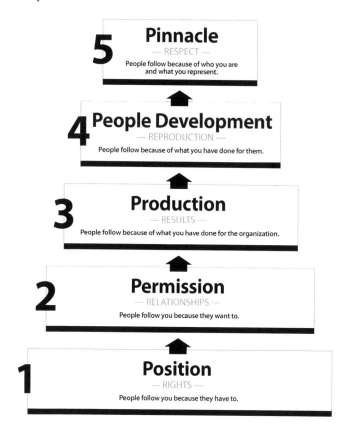

Level 5 Leadership – Jim Collins

Jim Collins in his book *Good to Great* also outlines 5 Levels of leadership that he has seen in many companies. This is just another way to look at leadership development and helping leaders grow.

The first step is their ability to identify and include the right people with them toward achieving goals. Unlike the traditional method of building strategies and then looking for the right people to carry them out, they take a different route. It's about getting the right people on board and then deciding on the destination.

1. They also do not shy away from facing and accepting brutal truths and realities of data, numbers, and situations. At the same time, they do not lose hope of a better future.
2. They also strive towards aligning consistent efforts towards a goal, rather than giving one massive push. They believe in small but firm pushes to bring in the momentum.
3. They also exercise their judgment to understand an aspect in-depth and thoroughly, rather than burdening themselves with myriad information.
4. They practice and encourage a disciplined approach toward their work-life and as visionaries use carefully identified technologies to give their businesses strategic advantage.

LEVEL 5

LEVEL 5 EXECUTIVE
Builds enduring greatness through a paradoxical blend of personal humility and professional will.

LEVEL 4

EFFECTIVE LEADER
Catalyzes commitment to and vigorous pursuit of a clear and compelling vision, stimulating higher performance standards.

LEVEL 3

COMPETENT MANAGER
Organizes people and resources toward the effective and efficient pursuit of predetermined objectives.

LEVEL 2

CONTRIBUTING TEAM MEMBER
Contributes individual capabilities to the achievement of group objectives and works effectively with others in a group setting.

LEVEL 1

HIGHLY CAPABLE INDIVIDUAL
Makes productive contributions through talent, knowledge, skills, and good work habits.

5 Levels of Leadership (a more in-depth explanation from John Maxwell)

You are a leader. But where are you on your leadership journey, and where do you go from here? Over my years of teaching about leadership, that question exists at the heart of so many leaders. Everyone wants to know where they stand and how to get to the next level. And you are probably no different!

That's why I developed the 5 Levels of Leadership paradigm in my book, Developing the Leader Within You, and then expanded it in my book, The 5 Levels of Leadership. I wanted to help leaders understand and increase their effectiveness. And while there is more to this teaching than space in this blog, today I want to offer a general overview of the 5 Levels as a reminder that you are still on your way as a leader—and so am I!

THE 5 LEVELS OF LEADERSHIP
Level 1 — Position

The lowest level of leadership—the entry-level, if you will— is Position. It's the only level that requires no ability or effort to achieve. After all, anyone can be appointed to a position! While nothing is wrong with having a leadership position, everything is wrong with relying only on that position to get people to follow. That's because it only works if you have leverage (such as job security or a paycheck) over your followers. At Level 1, people only follow if they believe that they have to.

People who remain on the position level may find it difficult to work with volunteers. Why? Because position does not automatically result in influence, volunteers are aware that they don't have to follow anyone. They truly only follow if they want to.

But the news is not all bad about this level. It is a prime place for you to begin investing in your growth and potential as a leader. Use your time at this level of learning to lead yourself—through priorities and self-discipline—and you'll be ready to move to the next level.

Level 2 — Permission

Level 2 is based on relationships. At this level, people choose to follow because they want to. In other words, they give the leader Permission to lead them. To grow at this level, leaders work on getting to know their people and connecting with them. You can't lead without people, which means you need to learn to like people if you want to lead well!

When you like people and treat them as individuals who have value, you begin to develop positive influence with them. Trust grows, which usually leads to respect. And the environment becomes much more positive—whether at home, on the job, at play, or while volunteering. Level 2 is where solid, lasting relationships are built that create the foundation for the next level.

Level 3 — Production

The best leaders know how to motivate their people to GTD—get things done! And getting things done is what Level 3 is all about. On this level, leaders who produce results build their influence and credibility. People still follow because they want to, but they do it because of more than the relationship. People follow Level 3 leaders because of their track record.

The Production level is where leaders can become change agents. Work gets done, morale improves, profits go up, turnover goes down, and goals are achieved. The more you produce, the more you're able to tackle tough problems and face thorny issues. Leading and influencing others becomes fun because when everyone is moving forward together, the team rises to another level of effectiveness.

It's important to note here that the goal with the 5 Levels is not to move away from one level to grow at a new level. Instead, these 5 levels of leadership build upon each other. In other words, Level 3 leaders still need to do the things that make Level 2 happen. They just add Level 3 strategies to the mix. And as they become effective at Level 3, they are ready to layer on the goals of the next levels.

Level 4 — People Development

Level 4 can be summed up in one word: reproduction. *Your goal at this level is to identify and develop as many leaders as you can by investing in them and helping them grow.*

The reason is simple: When there are more leaders, more of the organization's mission can be accomplished. The people you choose to develop may show great leadership potential, or they may be diamonds in the rough, but the main idea is the same: When you invest in them, you can reproduce yourself.

The more you raise new leaders, the more you will change the lives of all members of the team. As a result, people will follow you because of what you've done for them. And as a bonus, some of those mentoring relationships are likely to last a lifetime. So, to grow at the people development level, you need to make investing in leaders a priority, and take intentional steps every day to help them grow. Do that consistently, for long enough, and you may begin to reap the rewards of the next level.

Level 5 — Pinnacle

The highest level of leadership is also the most challenging to attain. It requires longevity as well as intentionality. You simply can't reach Level 5 unless you are willing to invest your life into the lives of others for the long haul. But if you stick with it, if you continually focus on both growing yourself at every level and developing leaders who are willing and able to develop other leaders, you may find yourself at the Pinnacle.

The commitment to becoming a Pinnacle leader is seizable, but so are the payoffs. Level 5 leaders develop Level 5 organizations. They create opportunities other leaders don't. They create a legacy in what they do. People follow them because of who they are and what they represent. In other words, their leadership gains a positive reputation. As a result, Level 5 leaders often transcend their position, their organization, and sometimes their industry.

There's so much more I'd love to tell you but let me leave you

with this. Leadership is about growth – for yourself, your relation-
ships, your productivity, and your people. To lead well, you must
embrace your need for continual improvement, and the 5 Levels
provide a leadership GPS to help you with your journey. You must
know where you are, to know where you're going. Otherwise, as
the Cheshire Cat told Alice, when you don't know where you're go-
ing, any road will get you there.

The following are reflections and insights from John Maxwell's *5 Levels of Leadership*.

1. Remain humble and teachable.
2. Maintain your core focus.
3. Create the right inner circle to keep you grounded.
4. Do what only you can do.
5. Create a supercharged leadership development environment.
6. Create room at the top.
7. Develop your top leaders.
8. Plan your succession and your legacy.
9. Use your leadership success as a platform for something greater.

Insights into the 5 Levels – Maxwell shares 10 insights that help the reader understand how the levels are related:

1. You can move up a level, but you never leave the previous one behind.
2. You are not on the same level with every person.
3. The higher you go, the easier it is to lead.
4. The higher you go, the more time and commitment is required to win a level.
5. Moving up levels occurs slowly, but going down can happen quickly.
6. The higher you go, the greater the return.
7. Moving farther up always requires further growth.
8. Not climbing the levels limits you and your people.

9. When you change positions or organizations, you seldom stay at the same level.

10. You cannot climb the levels alone.

3 Perspectives of Leadership Development

5 Levels of Leadership John Maxwell	Level 5 Leadership Jim Collins	The Coaching Leader Leadership Skill Development
1. **Position** – People follow because they have to. Define your Leadership. Shift from Position to Potential. Focus on the Vision. Shift from Rules to Relationships.	**Highly Capable Individual** Highly capable individuals or regular workers who are talented, knowledgeable, and skilled. They are effective in the workplace.	**Lead Self – Personal/ Self-Leadership** Character (integrity and humility) Self-Aware (personality, gifts, talents, experience, strengths) Servant Leadership Time Management Own It – take responsibility Choosing to Think and Feel Effectively Self-Confidence, Self-Efficacy
2. **Permission** – People follow because they want to. Side by Side, Initiation, Servanthood. Development, Encouragement. Innovation. Relationships alone are not enough.	**Contributing Team Member** Contributing team members are good at working with others and are notably proficient at helping their groups reach objectives.	**Lead Others** Trust Culture Excellence Mindset Role Knowledge and Effectiveness

3. Production – People follow because of what you have done for the organization. Understand how your giftedness contributes to the vision. Cast vision for what needs to be accomplished. Begin to develop your people into a team. Prioritize the things that yield a high return. Be willing and ready to be a change agent. Keep focused that results are the goal.	**Competent Manager** Competent managers can effectively oversee people and resources, helping to achieve predetermined goals.	**Lead Skillfully** Vision Casting Leadership Team Strategy Thinking Delegation Planning Alignment Change Management
4. People Development – People follow because of what you have done for them. Be willing to keep growing yourself. Decide that people are worth the effort. Work through your insecurities. Recruit the best people to develop. Commit to spending the time to develop. Create a personal development process. Never work alone. Blend the soft and hard sides of development. Take responsibility for energizing others.	**Effective Leader** Effective leaders can steer their companies toward well-defined compelling goals. They also keep their organizations functioning at high levels of performance.	**Lead Teams** Delegate / Empower Communication Conflict Resolution Lead According to Need **People Development** Coach Promote *"The ultimate leader is willing to develop people to the point that they eventually surpass him or her in knowledge and ability."* **— Fred Manske Jr.**

5. Pinnacle – People follow because of who you are and what you represent. Make room for others at the top. Continually mentor potential Level 5 leaders. Create an inner circle that will keep you grounded—"those closest to leaders determine their potential." Do things for the organization. Plan for your succession—leave a positive legacy—make the right decisions along the way.	**Executive** Executives have the unique capability to develop a company's greatness through a paradox of personal humility plus professional will.	**Lead Organizations** Culture Development Engagement Meeting Cadence and Accountability **Sustain – Scale – Multiply** Leadership Succession Future of Organization Is Secure

The Coaching Leader – Leadership Skill Development

The focus here is to outline specific leadership skills that are found at each level of leadership and to begin work on understanding and application. A key application of *The Coaching Leader* is for you as a leader to become skilled at developing the people around you to be more effective and fruitful as leaders. This idea helps you assess where you and those around are and what it will take in terms of skills and actions to move to the next level.

From this outline – assess where you are:

- The 5 Levels of Leadership – what stage? What does it look like? How can you move forward?

- Level 5 Leadership – what stage? What does it look like? How can you move forward?

- The Coaching Leader Skills – What skills are you proficient in? Where do you need to grow? What skills lie ahead?

Outline a simple plan for the next three to six months to work on moving to the next level on either scale. What one or two skills might you want to work on?

Chapter Ten

COACHING MATTERS

In this chapter we cover a number of topics that relate to coaching and helping the coachee in specific ways to increase effectiveness. We will cover issues that relate to the coachee and the leader as coach, and then process issues.

Coachee
> Knowing the Person
> Helping Leaders Take Responsibility
> Time Management, Do Delegate Dump

Coach
> Backbone and Heart

Process
> Meeting Cadence and Connection
> Handling Challenges and Conflict
> Leading Change
> Lead According to Need
> Coaching Questions

Coachee – Knowing the Person

As a coach, getting to know the coachee is extremely critical. We all have unique personalities and are wired differently. Who we are shapes the things we like and how we tend to do things. We will explore several facets of this and how it can enhance the effectiveness of coaching.

Relationships

To be effective at coaching, it is imperative to build a strong relationship between you as the coach and the coachee. It's in these relationships that the real issues and the underlying challenges come to the surface. It's also in these relationships that we get to know the person in a deeper way—their purpose, dreams, cares, concerns, and emotions. We get to know who people are and how they like to do things.

Valuing Each Other

When one has a good and growing relationship with another, they can begin to truly value them as a person and not for just what they do. As a coach you need to believe the best about people in order to truly value them. When a coachee feels valued, they will be more committed to the process and feel better about themselves.

Personality

A key tool that is extremely useful in the coaching process is a personality instrument that gives an understanding of a person's wiring and innate make-up. Several tools could be used with great confidence and are highly recommended. Which tool to use and the plus/minus of each is beyond the purpose of this book. Here are four instruments or assessments that have significant acclaim and usage.

- DiSC
- Myers – Briggs – MBTI
- Gallup StrengthFinders
- 5 Voices

Strengths/Gifts/Talents

Strengths are those actions we take that we can do very well without a significant amount of effort. Again, taking an inventory of one's strengths and then working in these areas is very helpful.

Every individual has gifts and talents that help shape and direct their life and work. Taking an inventory and exploring these will also be helpful in the coaching process. So, what can you do? In the coaching conversation, ask some follow-up questions that explore their strengths and potential weaknesses. Knowing these strengths helps in three key areas.

1. **Personal Management and Leading Yourself**
    - Shapes your purpose.
    - Increases your engagement and satisfaction, joy.
    - Affirms strengths as a gift.
    - Enhances communication and relationships with the body.
    - Connects your action and give perspective.

2. **Work Performance**
    - Increases engagement.
    - Enhances communications.
    - A means of affirming and appreciating other gifts.
    - Aligns task and personality.

3. **Teamwork**

    Leverages work – aligns more to strengths.

    Engages every person more effectively.

    Recruits to needs.

    Deepens relationships.

Strengths-Based Cultures Are Vital to the Future of Work by Steve Crabtree

Employees who say they use their strengths every day are 8% more productive and 15% less likely to quit their jobs. They are also more likely to strongly agree that they like what they do each day. Employees need continual learning and development opportunities to stay up to date. Understanding their strengths gives them a basis for choosing the developmental paths that are most likely to help them sustain a long, successful career.

From the standpoint of individual employees, then, a strengths foundation that includes coaching and development provides a sense of their "true north"—helping them stay oriented for high productivity amid shifting workplace needs and varying career trajectories. But as more businesses restructure their pro-

cesses around team-based work, the benefits of a strengths-based culture for group interactions also becomes more important.

Team members who know each other's strengths more effectively relate to one another, avoiding potential conflicts and boosting group cohesion. Strengths-based development immediately changes their conversations. It creates more positive dialogue, and it boosts the team's overall engagement and performance.

Leaders who become more like coaches help team members understand and cultivate their talents, thereby achieving high levels of productivity and fulfillment. This change aligns with research by Gallup and others showing that younger workers—particularly millennials—want and expect their managers to work with them on personal and professional development opportunities.

— **Steve Crabtree** is a senior editor and research analyst for Gallup. He is the lead editor of Gallup's State of the Global Workplace reports.

Helping Leaders Take Responsibility

"A sign of wisdom and maturity is when you come to terms with the realization that your decisions cause your rewards and consequences. You are responsible for your life, and your ultimate success depends on the choices you make." — **Denis Waitley**

"Man must cease attributing his problems to his environment and learn again to exercise his will—his personal responsibility."
— **Albert Einstein**

Leaders have responsibilities that are expected of them. This is a critical characteristic that coaches must help the coachee embrace and master. Like discipline, responsibility is one of the most important things to grow in since it makes you more productive in life. Without this as a foundation, one can have the talents and gifting, yet it will count for nothing because there is little to no follow-through. Here are six aspects of discipline that will help you grow in your responsibility and self-control.

1. **There is always a price to pay.**

"Liberty means responsibility. That is why most men dread it."
— George Bernard Shaw

   Not taking responsibility may be less demanding, less painful, and mean less time spent in the unknown. It's more comfortable. You can just take it easy and blame problems in your life on someone else. But there is always a price to pay. When you don't take responsibility for your life, you give away your personal power.

2. **Build your self-esteem.**

"Disciplining yourself to do what you know is right and important, although difficult, is the high road to pride, self-esteem, and personal satisfaction." **— Brian Tracy**

"The willingness to accept responsibility for one's own life is the source from which self-respect springs." **— Joan Didion**

   Why do people often have self-esteem problems? I'd say that one of the big reasons is that they don't take responsibility for their lives. Instead, someone else is blamed for the bad things that happen and a victim mentality is created and empowered. This damages many vital parts of your life—stuff like relationships, ambitions, and achievements. That hurt will not stop until you wise up and take responsibility for your life. There is no way around it.

   Just try it out. You feel so much better about yourself even if you only take personal responsibility for your own life for a day. This is also a way to stop relying on external validation like praise from other people to feel good about yourself. Instead, you start building stability within and a sort of inner spring that fuels your life with positive emotions no matter what other people say or do around you. This brings us to the next reason to take personal responsibility...

3. **Taking action becomes natural.**

"Action springs not from thought, but from a readiness for responsibility." **— Dietrich Bonhoeffer**

It is often said that your thoughts become your actions. But without taking responsibility for your life, those thoughts often just stay on that mental stage and aren't translated into action. Taking responsibility for your life is that extra ingredient that makes taking action more of a natural thing. You don't get stuck in just thinking, thinking, and wishing so much. You become proactive instead of passive.

4. **Understand the limits of your responsibility.**

   "Make the best use of what is in your power and take the rest as it happens." — **Epictetus**

   Taking responsibility for your life is great. But that is also all that you have control over. You can't control the results of your actions. You can't control how someone reacts to what you say or what you do. It's important to know where your limits are. Otherwise, you'll create a lot of unnecessary suffering for yourself and waste energy and focus by taking responsibility for what you can't and never really could control.

5. **Don't forget to take responsibility in everyday life too.**

   "I long to accomplish a great and noble task, but it is my chief duty to accomplish small tasks as if they were great and noble." **— Helen Keller**

   "You cannot escape the responsibility of tomorrow by evading it today." — **Abraham Lincoln**

   Life consists of each day, not just the big events sometime in the future. So, don't forget to take responsibility for the little things today too. Don't postpone it. Taking responsibility for your life can be hard and taxing on you. It's not something you master over the weekend. So, you might as well get started with it right now.

6. **Aim to be your best self.**

   "Hold yourself responsible for a higher standard than anybody expects of you. Never excuse yourself." — **Henry Ward Beecher**

"Peak performance begins with your taking complete responsibility for your life and everything that happens to you." — **Brian Tracy**

This is of course not easy. But it's a lot of fun and the payoff is massive.

- **You are not trying to escape from your life anymore.** Instead, you take control, face what's going on and so the world and new options open up for you.

- **You start taking action not just when you feel like it.** Improvement isn't about short spurts once in a while. Consistent action is what really pays off and can help you achieve just about anything.

- **You build your self-esteem to higher levels.** You may discover that many smaller problems you experience regularly such as negative thinking, self-defeating behavior, and troubled relationships with yourself and others start to correct themselves as your self-esteem improves. You gain an inner stability and can create your own positive feelings within without the help of validation from other people.

So how do you take responsibility? Well, it's simply a choice that you have to make. Reviewing the reasons above—and now also the awesome quotes—is for me a powerful way to keep myself in line, though it doesn't always work. Doing the right thing in every situation is hard to do and also hard to always keep in mind. So, don't aim for perfection, aim to learn, grow, and improve continually.

When you know those very important reasons above, it becomes a lot easier to stick with taking responsibility. And to not rationalize to yourself that you didn't have to take responsibility in various situations. That doesn't mean that I beat myself up endlessly about it. I just observe that I have hurt myself and my life. And that doesn't feel good. And so, I become less prone to repeat the same mistake.

(http://www.positivityblog.com/index.php/2009/03/13/7-time-less-thoughts-on-taking-responsibility-for-your-life/)

Time Management

Time management leads to great strategy and keeping priorities.

A key aspect of coaching is to help the coachee use their time wisely. The following tools help you identify and focus on the highest and best use of one's time.

Practice: Urgent/Important Principle

To achieve excellence and results, you must use time effectively, not just efficiently.

Time stressors are some of the most pervasive sources of pressure in the workplace, and they happen as a result of having too much to do in too little time. So, how can you beat this stress, and deliver the things that are essential to doing a good job? Eisenhower's Urgent/Important Principle helps you think about your priorities and determine which of your activities are important and which are, essentially, distractions.

What Are "Urgent" and "Important" Activities?

In a 1954 speech to the Second Assembly of the World Council of Churches, U.S. President Dwight D. Eisenhower, who was quoting Dr. J. Roscoe Miller, president of Northwestern University, said: "I have two kinds of problems: the urgent and the important. The urgent are not important, and the important are never urgent." This "Eisenhower Principle" is said to be how he organized his workload and priorities.

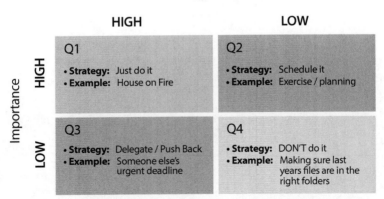

Urgency

	HIGH	LOW
HIGH (Importance)	**Q1** • **Strategy:** Just do it • **Example:** House on Fire	**Q2** • **Strategy:** Schedule it • **Example:** Exercise / planning
LOW (Importance)	**Q3** • **Strategy:** Delegate / Push Back • **Example:** Someone else's urgent deadline	**Q4** • **Strategy:** DON'T do it • **Example:** Making sure last years files are in the right folders

He recognized that great time management means being effective as well as efficient. In other words, we must spend our time on things that are important and not just the ones that are urgent. To do this, and to minimize the stress of having too many tight deadlines, we need to understand this distinction:

	Urgent	Not Urgent
Important	**I** » Crises » Pressing problems » Firefighting » Major scrap and rework » Deadline-driven projects	**II** » Prevention » *Production capability* activities » Relationship building » Recognizing new opportunities » Planning » *Re*-creation
Not Important	**III** » Interruptions » Some calls » Some mail » Some reports » Some meetings » Proximate pressing matters » Popular activities » Some scrap & rework	**IV** » Trivia » Busywork » Some mail » Some phone calls » Time-wasters » Pleasant activities

1. **Important** activities have an outcome that leads to us achieving our goals, whether these are professional or personal.

2. **Urgent** activities demand immediate attention and are usually associated with achieving someone else's goals. They are often the ones we concentrate on, and they demand attention because the consequences of not dealing with them are immediate.

When we know which activities are important and which are urgent, we can overcome the natural tendency to focus on unimportant urgent activities so that we can clear enough time to do what's essential for our success. This is the way we move from "firefighting" into a position where we can grow our businesses and our careers.

How to Use Eisenhower's Principle

1. Important and Urgent   MANAGE IT: ASSESS – Do or Delegate
2. Important but not Urgent   FOCUS – Be Strategic
3. Not Important but Urgent   DELEGATE
4. Not Important and not Urgent   LIMIT – AVOID

Eisenhower's Urgent/Important Principle helps you quickly identify the activities that you should focus on, as well as the ones you should ignore.

When you use this tool to prioritize your time, you can deal with truly urgent issues at the same time as you work towards important, longer-term goals. Outline in each category the top 3-5 issues you are currently facing.

Assess / Analyze / Act

	URGENT	NOT URGENT
IMPORTANT	**Q1** *Manage / Assess: Do or Delegate*	**Q2** *Focus*
NOT IMPORTANT	**Q3** *Delegate*	**Q4** *Limit / Avoid*

Coach

In her book, *Executive Coaching*, Mary Beth O'Neill discusses this idea with the description of coaching with backbone and heart.

Coaching with Backbone and Heart – Mary Beth O'Neil

"Leadership maturity drives alignment, and alignment drives outstanding results. This requires transforming how you show up to lead. The secret to leadership maturity is how well you embody and balance "backbone and heart" as you face the four choice points with your team. As a leader, you are challenged to: 1) choose your stance, AND 2) value others' interests as much as your own, and then 3) use your authority to decide or delegate appropriately, and ensure that others resolve their reservations to commitment. What is most often missing when leaders fail is the thoughtful use of this kind of direct interaction as a practice. Only through these mature interactions can you address important issues of conflict and authority, and create committed, well-coordinated leadership teams that cascade that alignment throughout the rest of your organization."

Backbone *is having the nerve to –*

- *Choose your course, especially in controversial situations.*
- *Take a clear, non-anxious position with others about your goals and expectation.,*
- *Either hold your position even when people are anxious about your decision, or choose to be influenced by others' positions because you think they serve the outcomes best.*

Heart *is having the nerve to –*

- *Be interested in others' positions.*
- *Encourage others' interests and participation.*
- *Invite their participation both when they agree and when they disagree with you.*
- *Empathize with their frustration and disappointment when you decide against their interests.*

Speak the Truth in Love

As a coaching leader, we are called to speak the truth in love. This means we give an accurate and clear picture of what the reality is but we do it with grace and care for the individual as not to crush them. People deserve the respect of hearing truth that might address a blind spot or an area of growth in a way that helps them grow rather than put them down. It is the mature coaching leader that finds the right blend that helps the individual grow and welcome this kind of approach.

Be Direct and Listen at the Same Time

This mature skill of being an effective coaching leader combines both being direct and straightforward and yet taking the time to listen and gather all of the facts. They don't jump to conclusions, nor do they put things under the carpet and leave issues unaddressed.

Empowered and Accountable

Another aspect of this maturity is shown in the coaching process when a leader empowers people. In other words, they give people the appropriate authority and responsibility but also hold them accountable. We have addressed accountability previously, but it's simply the idea that we inspect what we expect. This shows respect to the individual, because you want to help them grow, but it also reinforces that results are important and need to be accomplished.

PROCESS
Handling Challenges and Conflict

Conflict Coaching (Adapted from Peacemakers)

When someone asks for your help in resolving a conflict, you can often do a great deal of good without getting directly involved in the dispute. Instead, you can simply offer counsel on how that individual might be able to go back to the other person and resolve their differences in private. This process of offering individual counsel is sometimes referred to as "coaching," because the conciliator is offering encouragement and advice from the sidelines instead of getting directly involved with both parties in the dispute.

An effective coach will listen carefully and promote personal responsibility while guiding individuals through the basic steps of resolution.

Conflict can make life very awkward. It often catches us off guard and leads us to say and do things we later regret. When someone offends us, we often react without thinking. Soon it is as if we are sliding down a slippery slope and things are going from bad to worse.

Escape Responses

Two responses are commonly used by people who are more interested in avoiding or getting away from a conflict than resolving it.

- **Denial**—One way to escape from a conflict is to pretend that no problem exists. Another way is to refuse to do what should be done to resolve a conflict properly.
- **Flight**—Another way to escape from a conflict is to run away.

Attack Responses

These responses are often used by people who are more interested in winning a conflict than in preserving a relationship.

- **Assault**—Some people try to overcome an opponent by using various forms of force or intimidation, such as verbal attacks (including gossip and slander), physical violence, or efforts to damage a person. Such conduct usually escalates the conflict.
- **Litigation**—Some conflicts may legitimately be taken before a civil judge.

Conciliation Responses

The three responses of Conciliation are directed at finding a just and mutually agreeable solution to a conflict.

- **Reconciliation**—If an offense is too serious to overlook or has damaged our relationship, we need to resolve personal or relational issues through confession, loving correction, and forgiveness.
- **Negotiation**—Even if we successfully resolve relational issues, we may still need to work through material issues related to money, property, or other rights. This should be done through a cooperative bargaining process in which you and the other person seek to reach a settlement that satisfies the legitimate needs of each side.

- **Mediation**—If two people cannot reach an agreement in private, they should ask one or more objective outside people to meet with them to help them communicate more effectively and explore possible solutions.

As you can see, the escape responses only postpone a proper solution to a problem, and attack responses usually damage relationships and make conflicts worse. Therefore, you should generally try first to deal with conflict personally and privately by using one of the three conciliation responses.

When people are faced with conflict, it is natural to try to escape from the situation or to attack the other party. Escape responses only postpone a proper solution to a problem, and attack responses usually damage relationships and make conflicts worse. Therefore, you should generally guide people away from these responses and encourage them to respond to deal with conflict in private by using a conciliation response.

If repeated efforts at personal peacemaking do not resolve a dispute, you may need to help the person implement one of the other conciliation responses (mediation or arbitration)

Show How Conflict Is an Opportunity

A person's attitude powerfully affects the way he or she responds to conflict. Therefore, it is important to help people see that conflict is not necessarily bad or destructive. Coaches serve other people by helping them to bear their burdens or by confronting them in love.

Listen Carefully and Dig for Information

The greatest drawback to conflict coaching is that you are getting only one side of the story. Instead of jumping to conclusions and offering hasty advice, give people time to fully explain their situation. Then ask careful questions to fill in the gaps in their story and learn how they may have contributed to the conflict through their own attitudes, words, or actions. Only after you have understood as much of the situation as possible should you begin to suggest ways that people can pursue peace, and even then you should resist drawing any final conclusions about people with whom you have not talked.

Promote Personal Responsibility

A good coach doesn't run the plays for the players. Your job is to provide wise counsel and develop sound plans, but then you need to stand back and let the person you are advising put the plan into action.

This role distinction is especially important because people in conflict are often looking for someone to solve their problems for them. If you give in to that desire, you will usually end up with superficial, temporary solutions.

Therefore, while you should certainly do what is necessary to help people deal with matters that are truly beyond their abilities, you should be careful not to take over their responsibilities. One way to help people take ownership of the solution to their problems is to give them specific assignments.

Provide the "Three P's" of Satisfaction

As you mediate a dispute, you should strive to provide the parties with three types of satisfaction.

- **Process satisfaction** results from providing the parties with a fair, orderly, and even-handed process that gives everyone involved a reasonable opportunity to present the information they believe is relevant to the dispute.

- **Personal satisfaction** results from consistently treating the parties with respect, courtesy, and equality.

- **Product satisfaction** results from leading the parties to a final solution that is perceived as being just and equitable, both substantively and personally. It is important to note that in the long run, most parties place as much value on the process and personal satisfaction as they do on product satisfaction. (This is true even though they usually devote most of their energy to achieving a particular outcome.)

The fact that parties value process and personal satisfaction is good news because a mediator usually has much more control over these things than the final outcome of a dispute. By carefully providing the parties with a fair process and treating them with genuine respect, you can usually achieve a durable agreement and a high degree of satisfaction, even when the final solution is not entirely to everyone's liking.

Meeting Cadence and Connection

We have covered the four broad areas of known as the Core 4 Framework in terms of four big ideas. This lays a great foundation of input and information, yet how and when do we do all this planning and having conversations which are critical to execution? We will look at four areas: Assessments, Planning, Meetings, and Reviews.

Annual Assessments

These two assessments should be done annually, maybe at the end of year or the beginning the new year, to give you a picture and basis on which to do your planning.

PERSONAL	Life Synergy Assessment
FUNCTIONAL	Work Performance and Results – The Five Factor Assessment

Annual Planning

Much like the assessments, there is an annual component to planning which should also take place on an annual basis. There are essentially three areas to focus on: personal. Work performance and professional development.

- **One-Page Development Plan** – this includes the Life Synergy planning for personal. It incorporates a life purpose.

These next two tools and forms accomplish the same primary thing which is to have an annual Work Performance Plan with a well thought through process and assessment that establishes goals and agreed upon outcomes.

- **Work Performance and Results – Planning**
- **Work Performance and Results – Goal Action Plan**

The third area is professional development which focuses on areas of growth that would include skills and competencies that will help you as a leader to be continually effective and add value.

Meeting Cadence

In terms of ongoing meetings, we are primarily focusing on the work environment.

- **Annual Meetings** – These meetings review yearly goals and action plans and so are usually held at the beginning of the year.
- **Quarterly Check-ups** – These meetings are to make sure that the performance is on track to reach the annual goals. It should include progress reports, resources needed, and any course corrections for both personal and for performance. The annual goals should be broken up into quarterly targets or "rocks."
- **Weekly, Bi-weekly, or Monthly progress/coaching meetings.** These meetings are check-ins to catch up on any burning issues and accountability on accomplishing the tasks needed to accomplish the quarterly targets. It also would address any issues that are preventing you from reaching your goals.

Reviews

There are three types of reviews: Annual Performance Reviews, Career Fit – 6 P's Conversations, and Purpose. We briefly review the focus of each of these reviews here. In the next chapter we will give you some actual tools, processes, and assessments to use.

- **Annual Performance Review** – This is an annual review to go over what was accomplished and how the work process went for the year. There should be no surprises in this type of meeting, and it should be documented. There are numerous examples and forms online from which to develop your own Annual Performance Review. Each company is different in how they look at and review their workers. We have included a sample from HR 360 Inc. *(https://www.hr360.com/Forms-and-Policies/Employee-or-HR-Notices-and-Requests/Employee-Evaluation-Form.aspx)*
- **Career Fit – 6 P's Conversation** – This is generally an annual conversation that helps determine the individual's fit in the role and in the organization to make sure people are in the right seats doing the highest and best things.

- **Purpose** – A purpose review should be done annually after it has been written and established.

Leading Change

The Change Process

"If you stop growing, you are dying. It is not the perfection of your life, but rather the direction."

Sustainable change is more than a function of coaching conversations and goal setting. If change is to last, what's talked about in the coaching sessions must extend into the everyday life of the employee. This should include support structures for change that the employee will need to have in place as they pursue their growth agenda. Effective coaches will help employees find ways to resource change, both inside and outside of the coaching sessions. Some of those resources may be directly related to the coach, and some will not be.

Why don't people change and grow?

1. They don't want to change.
2. They have a fear of failure or don't feel courageous enough.
3. Their environment is holding them back.

Ken Blanchard (2003) identifies seven reactions people have to change.

1. People will feel awkward, ill at ease, and self-conscious when confronted by change.
2. People will feel alone even if everyone else is going through the same change.
3. People will think first about what they have to give up.
4. People will think they can only handle so much change at once.
5. People will be concerned they don't have enough resources (time, money, skills) to implement the change.
6. People will be at different levels of readiness for any particular change.
7. If pressure is taken off, people will revert to old behaviors.

How do I change?

Framework for Change and Growth: FORCE > RESISTANCE = Change

Force = Vision x Motivation x Plan x Trust   V x M x P x T > R = Change

V = Vision: seeing and receiving reality (see life now and the future possibilities).

M = Motivation: positive passion and values or dissatisfaction with how things are now.

P = Plan: daily steps and a plan applied consistently that can be taken towards a vision.

T = Trust: speed of trust equals the speed of the team.

R = Resistance: the barriers to change.

Change is an inside-out process. Take time and discuss the four Force Factors of change. What are the specifics of each factor? Rate them on a scale of 1-10 in how effective or complete they are. Begin to work to increase each of the factors as you decrease the resistance or barriers.

7 Steps for an Effective Change Management Process

1. **Discern the Need.** Know the good to achieve or the problem to solve. Define the improvement. Create urgency. Leadership needs to clarify the why and vision.

2. **Team.** Bring the right people together and integrate the change process into culture and people.

3. **Vision.** Clarify the vision and prioritize the key objectives.

4. **Assessment.** Assess the 6 factors of change. Force and Resistance. Keep assessing the progress and adapt as needed. The assessment will shape the planning.

5. **Plan and Take Action.** Plan for the change – define who, what, and when for each of 4 elements for FORCE and the one element for RESISTANCE and CHANGE. Provide resources and measure progress. Provide the motivation. Delegate, empower. Take first steps. Keep the people engaged in the process.

6. **Communicate.** Communicate the progress on increasing the force and decreasing the resistance. Make adjustments. Involve all the layers of the organization.

7. **Celebrate.** Create quick wins. Solidify the wins in your culture. Celebrate. Keep focused on achieving the desired results.

Lead According to Need

"Different leadership styles are better in different situations, and leaders must be flexible enough to adapt their style to the situation they are in." **—Ken Blanchard, *Situational Leadership***

Coaching helps effective leaders to be versatile in being able to change their style according to the need of the team they are leading. There is no one right style because there are no right needs, there are many different needs. A good leader can change leadership styles as the situation changes.

The leadership that a parent offers to a child changes over time with the need of the child. So too, the leadership of a leader/manager to an employee changes according to the need and maturity of the person. It follows that the leader of a team must adapt according to the needs and maturity of the team.

The growth process for teams (and growing leaders) begins with a forming stage and moves to a functioning team, to an empowered team, and finally to a multiplying team. Different levels of team formation necessitate varying responses. As a leader seeks to build and grow their teams, they must "Lead according to Need." See the graphic on the next page.

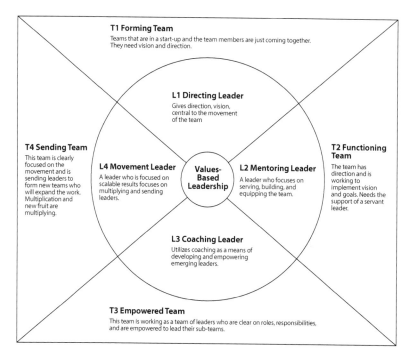

T1 Forming Team
Teams that are in a start-up and the team members are just coming together. They need vision and direction.

L1 Directing Leader
Gives direction, vision, central to the movement of the team

T4 Sending Team
This team is clearly focused on the movement and is sending leaders to form new teams who will expand the work. Multiplication and new fruit are multiplying.

L4 Movement Leader
A leader who is focused on scalable results focuses on multiplying and sending leaders.

Values-Based Leadership

L2 Mentoring Leader
A leader who focuses on serving, building, and equipping the team.

T2 Functioning Team
The team has direction and is working to implement vision and goals. Needs the support of a servant leader.

L3 Coaching Leader
Utilizes coaching as a means of developing and empowering emerging leaders.

T3 Empowered Team
This team is working as a team of leaders who are clear on roles, responsibilities, and are empowered to lead their sub-teams.

We will all have natural bents or styles as a leader. We all are wired in a certain way. We must not fall into the trap of "that is just how I lead." Every team is somewhere in this maturing process and where it is will shape how you lead. The right leadership style will be a primary means for the team to grow, mature, and become increasingly fruitful, able to move to the next level. Thus, how a leader leads the team will impact the results of the team.

Have you ever been part of a mature team where the leader struggled to delegate and did much of the work because it had to be just right? Or have you been part of a forming team that needed direction and the leader was trying to empower the team? In each of these cases, the style of the leader did not match the need of the team. How are you doing with your team— what is the primary need? How are you leading?

Consider the four styles of leadership: Directing, Mentoring, Coaching, and Multiplying and see how they correspond to the levels of team growth: Forming, Functioning, Empowered, and Sending.

You should assess your leadership and your team and engage with the appropriate action. When it comes to building a team, the actions need to shift and the coaching leader style is associated with that of an empowered team.

There is one absolute foundation in being able to "lead according to need" and that is humility. For a leader to adapt, they must put the team ahead of their style and choose to change. A humble leader cares about the needs of the team and people, allowing them to be in a position to serve.

The Coaching Leader: A Coaching Conversation

Learning to ask questions is critical to being an effective coach. The following is a framework for helping a coachee.

Set the Agenda & Goal:
- What do you want to be different, by when?
- Ask a few clarifying questions using the SMART goal framework (Specific, Measurable, Attainable, Relevant and Time-oriented).

Explore for Clarity & Insights:
- You mentioned _____. Tell me more about that!
- "How would you describe your attitude about these goals?"
- What success have you had in the past with doing something like this?
- What difficulties have you encountered?

As a coach, be paying attention to anything that seems significant: potential obstacles to success; listening for underlying beliefs, values, thoughts, and feelings that could undermine or help in how a coachee could accomplish the decision.

Generate Ideas & Options:
- What could you do?
- What else?
- "What ideas have you already thought of for seeing this need met?"
- "What else could you do?"
- "What else could you do?"

(Sometimes you keep asking the same question to cause the coachee to think and dig deeper.)

Decide & Focus:

- Which do you want to pursue?

When you have exhausted the potential ideas, challenge the coachee to consider the options they developed and have them choose those they most want to pursue.

Commit to Actions:

- What will you do?
- When will you do it?

Help them to determine and commit to some practical action steps related to the option they chose to pursue.

Check for Progress & Accountability:

- What progress did you make on your action steps?

Coaching is the art of asking questions that help a person discover deeper insights, greater awareness, and the opportunity to live more fully the life they were meant to live.

More Coaching Questions

Here are more questions that you might use for different situations.

Purpose questions:

- Why is it important to _____ to have this conversation today (for you, for the business, for the world)?
- From your perspective, what is our shared purpose today?
- What might get unlocked today in this symphony of strengths as we invite your collective intelligence to be revealed?
- What is an intention you want to set for today?
- What part of the solution do you want to play today?
- Why is it important for us to work on this today?
- Think of a time you adapted or have navigated change – What did you learn?

- What experience motivated you to attend this workshop?
- How do you want to be different at the end of this _____?

Future questions
- If you could imagine, how would you bring this strength into the future?
- Who would it impact?

Debrief questions:
- When have you seen a _____ – at its best?
- Where are you at your best?
- What can you notice?
- What did _____ make possible?
- If you are not noticing anything new, would you be open to remaining curious?
- Where could I really lean into this conversation?
- Can you look at this as a gift—you can experience it from a curious place and let's reflect on that afterwards.
- What are you hearing through the sharing?

Closing questions:
- What are 1-3 words to describe your experience _____ (today, moment, from exercise, etc)?
- Where have you seen _____?
- What is a commitment you can make as to how you will embody _____?
- What value did you see demonstrated by everyone today?
- How might you apply what you just learned?

Chapter Eleven

THE COACHING LEADER ASSESSMENTS AND EXERCISES

Personal – Life Planning Assessment

Coaching often begins with looking at our life before the work, as our lives are more than our work. When we look at life, the goal is to bring synergy to all areas of our lives, showing that the whole is greater than the parts. As you begin to coach someone in their life, the following are two different assessments or ways to look at this life synergy. As a coachee, it begins with understanding and then assessing yourself to see where you are and what are areas for improvement. Take the time to detail this and work this through, both as a coach and as a coachee. You could do one or both of these assessments to clearly see the synergy that can be the best you at work and for your future.

Guiding principles regarding...Personal – Life Synergy
- Those who discover and grow their Life Synergy enjoy having a whole, full, successful, and well-rounded life.
- It recognizes seven areas of life that must be addressed and worked on.
- This Life Synergy also has a mission that blends mission, vocation, profession, and passion.

Start with your Current Reality: Life Synergy Assessment
The key to finishing well is to be a person of character (good) and to

be faithful. Character embodies the idea of being trustworthy, honest, and walking with integrity. Faithfulness is simply doing everything you say you will do, what is mutually expected and agreed upon. People can count on us. We apply these to the seven areas of life.

1. Foundation of **Values** that guide your **Life Principles**.
2. Bring order to your **Money** and **Finances** to lay a foundation for freedom, peace, and service.
3. Clarify why you go to **Work** and how your **Purpose** produces direction and priorities.
4. Define true **Success** and **Significance** to empower your motivation and refine your motives.
5. Value **Relationships** and **Community** with love to create wholeness and give meaning to life.
6. Respond appropriately to life's **Circumstances** and **Challenges** because they will build or break you.
7. Handle your **Health** and B well to be generous with others and be fulfilled.

Exercise – Assess yourself

On a scale of 1-10 rate yourself in each of the seven areas:

1. _____ Having a foundation of personal **Values** and **Life Principles**.

2. _____ Bring order to your **Money** and **Finances** to lay a foundation for freedom and peace.

3. _____ Clarify why you go to **Work** and how your **Purpose** produces direction and priorities.

4. _____ Define true **Success** and **Significance** to empower your motivation and refine your motives.

5. _____ Value **Relationships** and **Community** with love to create wholeness and give meaning to life.

6. _____Respond appropriately to life's **Circumstances** and **Challenges** because they will build or break you.

7. _____Manage your **Health** and **Resources** in order to be generous with others and be fulfilled.

Where are your gaps? What is your greatest need as you reflect?

LIFE SYNERGY of Passion, Mission, Vocation, Profession

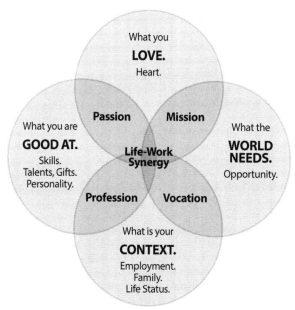

Having a healthy **Life Synergy** begins with having a personal mission in life that is beyond work and personal issues. It is a combination of mission, vocation, profession, and passion. It relates to doing what we love and intersecting that with what the world needs, what you're good at, and then what is the context of your work family and life status. As we find synergy in all areas and growth that is healthy, we will be about a personal mission that gives us a reason and a hope for living beyond the things of this world.

This activity is primarily owned by the individual and should be looked at 2-3 times per year or when there is a significant event. It would be helpful to share with your boss if life events were impacting your work performance effectiveness.

Once you have completed your assessment, it is recommended to do some life planning. The exercise and form for this planning is found on page 40 – One-Page Development Plan. Questions that will arise in this process may be something like:

- How are you doing at finding synergy in these areas?
- What plans or priorities emerge?
- What goals do you want to set and actions do you want to take going forward?

FUNCTIONAL – *Work Performance and Results – The Five Factor Assessment*

As a coach you want to help your coachee assess where they are in their work performance and results. The following Five Factor Assessment assists in that process as they look at leadership growth, business results, leadership behaviors, team interactions, and company culture. All of these may not apply, depending on what level of the organization you're at, but it is a comprehensive assessment that looks at the areas in terms of both needs and strengths and then begins to prioritize what are the most critical areas to start working on.

1. The leadership growth for you to achieve your purpose and life goals.
2. The business results that leaders need to achieve.
3. The leadership behaviors you need to exhibit.

4. The team interactions that the leader requires of staff in order to attain the desired results.

5. The company culture is healthy.

"It's simple but it's not easy."

50 Characteristics

For each heading or subheading identify 2 Needs (N) and 2 Strengths (S).

Five Factors Characteristics	Need / Strength	Priority
	N or S	Rate Top 5 N's and S's
LEADERSHIP GROWTH		
Clarified and written personal purpose		
Define life goals		
Possess a plan for work-life synergy and health		
Strengthen relational connections		
Know your personality type		
BUSINESS RESULTS		
Financial		
Sales		
Revenue		
Profit		
Expenses		
Product Cost		
ROI		
Strategic Direction		
Mission		
Vision		
Values		
Strategic Plan		
Alignment		
Customer Focus		

Excellence/Quality		
Meet Standards		
Excellence Mindset		
Defects		
Customer Satisfaction		
Innovation		
Operations		
Production, Finances, Services, Technology		
Customer Service		
Inventories		
Delivery		
Improvement		
LEADERSHIP BEHAVIORS		
Oversee the culture.		
Give goals and expectations.		
Ensure understanding.		
Gain commitment.		
Give corrective feedback.		
Acknowledge achievements.		
Develop next leaders.		
Has character to build trust.		
TEAM INTERACTIONS		
Level of trust		
Communication to clarify understanding		
Healthy giving thoughts, raising concerns		
Managing conflicts		
Clear roles and responsibilities		
Decision-making		
Accountability		
Own mistakes and initiate problem-solving		

Knowing strengths and applying them		
COMPANY CULTURE		
Has healthy environment of respect and mutual support.		
Mission, vision, and values are clear and lived out.		
There is a compelling strategic plan that is embraced.		
There is a growing, healthy trust.		
There is healthy conflict and conflict resolution.		
Leadership models the way.		

This assessment should be done at least once a year before working on your annual goals. It serves as a framework to consider the big picture and then to be able to establish a clearer picture of priorities.

- What Priorities Emerge?
- What action planning and goals do you want to tackle?

Work Performance and Results – Planning

The following chart helps us capture the specific coaching objectives in each of these five areas. You then define the goal that you're working on for the next three to six months as well as spelling out the action steps and the time it will take to get there.

Coaching Objectives	Goal – 90-120 days	Action Steps / Timing
LEADERSHIP - PERSONAL GROWTH		
BUSINESS RESULTS		

LEADERSHIP BEHAVIORS		
TEAM INTERACTIONS		
COMPANY CULTURE		

Begin writing out your **Goal Development Plan**.

Work Performance and Results – Goal Action Plan

The following chart is another tool you can use to record and monitor your goal action plans. The key is to simply write down the plan and begin to make progress. This tool helps keep you accountable as you measure your progress.

Guiding principles regarding…**Performance Management – Goals and Rocks**

- Individuals deserve **complete clarity regarding what's expected** of them in their roles (what success looks like).
- **Performance goals** should be defined, and **actual results** should be **measured in concrete terms**.
- Individuals need and want to **know how they are doing**, even if the feedback is "negative."
- Individuals expect performance to be evaluated in a **fair, predictable**, **consistent** and **accurate** manner.
- Individuals want to be **recognized and rewarded** based on the real **contributions** they make.

These development areas may include Leadership Skill Development, People Management, Communication, Time Management, Conflict Resolution, Strategic Planning Skills, etc.

Performance (Results) Goal Action Plan			
Roles and Responsibilities			
Goal – Metric Annual / Quarterly	**Action Steps**	**Timing**	**Resources needed**
Goal #1: *Importance:*			
Goal #2: *Importance:*			
Goal #3 *Importance:*			

Annual Performance Review – Employee Evaluation Form

I. EMPLOYEE INFORMATION	
Employee Name	Job Title
Supervisor/Reviewer	Review Period From: / / To: / /

II. CORE VALUES AND OBJECTIVES		
PERFORMANCE CATEGORY	RATING	COMMENTS AND EXAMPLES
Quality of Work: *Work is completed accurately (few or no errors), efficiently, and within deadlines with minimal supervision.*	❑ Exceeds expectations ❑ Meets expectations ❑ Needs improvement ❑ Unacceptable	
Attendance & Punctuality: *Reports for work on time; provides advance notice of need for absence.*	❑ Exceeds expectations ❑ Meets expectations ❑ Needs improvement ❑ Unacceptable	
Reliability/Dependability: *Consistently performs at a high level; manages time and workload effectively to meet responsibilities.*	❑ Exceeds expectations ❑ Meets expectations ❑ Needs improvement ❑ Unacceptable	
Communication Skills: *Written and oral communications are clear, organized, and effective; listens and comprehends well.*	❑ Exceeds expectations ❑ Meets expectations ❑ Needs improvement ❑ Unacceptable	
Judgment & Decision-Making: *Makes thoughtful, well-reasoned decisions; exercises good judgment, resourcefulness, and creativity in problem-solving.*	❑ Exceeds expectations ❑ Meets expectations ❑ Needs improvement ❑ Unacceptable	
Initiative & Flexibility: *Demonstrates initiative, often seeking out additional responsibility; identifies problems and solutions; thrives on new challenges and adjusts to unexpected changes.*	❑ Exceeds expectations ❑ Meets expectations ❑ Needs improvement ❑ Unacceptable	
Cooperation & Teamwork: *Is respectful of colleagues when working with others, and makes valuable contributions to help the group achieve its goals.*	❑ Exceeds expectations ❑ Meets expectations ❑ Needs improvement ❑ Unacceptable	

III. JOB-SPECIFIC PERFORMANCE CRITERIA

PERFORMANCE CATEGORY	RATING	COMMENTS AND EXAMPLES
Knowledge of Position: *Possesses required skills, knowledge, and abilities to competently perform the job.*	❑ Exceeds expectations ❑ Meets expectations ❑ Needs improvement ❑ Unacceptable	
Training & Development: *Continually seeks ways to strengthen performance, and regularly monitors new developments in field of work.*	❑ Exceeds expectations ❑ Meets expectations ❑ Needs improvement ❑ Unacceptable	

IV. PERFORMANCE GOALS

Set objectives and outline steps to improve in problem areas or further employee development.

V. OVERALL RATING

❑ EXCEEDS EXPECTATIONS	❑ MEETS EXPECTATIONS	❑ NEEDS IMPROVEMENT	❑ UNACCEPTABLE
Employee consistently performs at a high level that exceeds expectations.	*Employee satisfies all essential job requirements; may exceed expectations periodically; demonstrates likelihood of eventually exceeding expectations.*	*Employee consistently performs below required standards/expectations for the position; training or other action is necessary to correct performance.*	*Employee is unable or unwilling to perform required duties according to company standards; immediate improvement must be demonstrated.*

Comment on the employee's overall performance.

VI. EMPLOYEE COMMENTS (OPTIONAL)

VII. ACKNOWLEDGEMENT

I acknowledge that I have had the opportunity to discuss this performance evaluation with my manager/supervisor and I have received a copy of this evaluation.

Employee Signature: Date:

Reviewer Signature: Date:

Above sample from HR 360 Inc.
https://www.hr360.com/Forms-and-Policies/Employee-or-HR-Notices-and-Requests/Employee-Evaluation-Form.aspx

PROFESSIONAL – *Professional Development Plan – Growth and Advancement* (used with the permission of Lewis Leadership LLC)

The following professional development plan is a simple table that outlines goals or focus areas to work on. One then defines their objectives, vision of success, and barriers to success in the next three columns. Finally, there are specific action items and timing that the person proposes to take to accomplish their goals. This planning exercise is excellent both for the coach to guide the coachee and for the coachee to have a clear plan of action for which they can be held accountable.

Guiding principles regarding…**Professional Development**

- While development is related to performance, it should be approached differently than performance.
- To be effective, professional development must be "fully owned and managed" by the individual.
- Professional development focus areas should be established through collaboration with the employee's manager.
- Professional development should support both the employee's current job and longer-term career objectives.
- The company's and the manager's role in professional development is to provide an effective process, a supportive environment, and appropriate resources.
- Professional development must include personal work/life synergy and take into account life issues.

Professional Developmental Plan – PDP

Focus Area	Objective	Vision of Success	Barriers to Success	Specific Action Items/ Timing
[Enter the name of the area which you are trying to acquire, develop, improve, or correct.]	[Enter a one-sentence goal statement for each Focus Area that describes the result you are trying to achieve in each.]	[List bullet points that describe what you and others will be experiencing when you are fully accomplishing your objective for this Focus Area.]	[List bullet points that describe the specific reasons you have not been or may not be successful in achieving the Vision of Success in the previous column.]	
Goal 1				
Goal 2				
Goal 3				
Goal 4				

Career Fit – Direction (used with the permission of Lewis Leadership LLC)

The Career Fit or 6P Framework helps a person look at their life—especially their work life—and see where they are in terms of purpose, passion, proficiency, and preference in order to make sure that they are in the right seat doing the right things. This is an excellent exercise for a coach to use to help their coachee chart their career progress (usually on an annual basis) to make sure that they are in that right place and have a forward-looking plan for improvement.

Guiding principles regarding...**Career Management – 6P Framework**

- Career management begins with a clarity on life purpose and calling.
- In addition to success in their current roles, committed professionals also desire to continuously progress toward their long-term career aspirations.
- As with development, the individual is responsible to plan and manage their own career.
- As such, it is critical that individuals know themselves and what they aspire to achieve in life, both personally and professionally (6PGoal Setting).
- The individual should evaluate and select opportunities based on the best and highest personal and professional FIT.
- In the same way, an organization's willingness to offer a position to an individual depends on their assessment of the individual's FIT with the role.
- To correctly decide on FIT, both parties must mutually define, apply, and evaluate the correct FIT criteria (6Ps – Aligning to Ensure the Right Fit).

6P Framework – Six Levels of Alignment
(Lewis Leadership LLC)

Guiding Principles
- Committed professionals desire to progress toward their long-term career aspirations.

- The <u>individual</u> is responsible to <u>plan and manage their own career</u>.
- It is critical to <u>know yourself</u> and your aspirations <u>both personally and professionally</u>.
- <u>A means of evaluating and selecting opportunities</u> about the <u>best and highest personal & professional FIT</u>.
- <u>Facilitates an organization's willingness</u> to offer a position <u>depending on individual's FIT</u> with the role.
- Mutually <u>defines, applies, and evaluates the correct FIT criteria</u> (6Ps of Alignment).

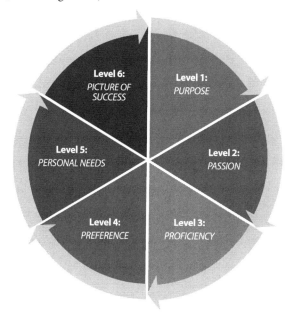

Level 1: PURPOSE

As individuals, each of us has a sense of a personal purpose or "calling" regarding the kind of life we want to live—spiritually, relationally, personally, and vocationally—and the environment in which we want to live it. Whether we are aware or not, this sense of purpose is grounded in a set of personal values and deeply held beliefs that we hold as very important, if not inviolate. Therefore, it is critical to our long-term satisfaction that the organization we are part of represent a purpose (the reason it exists), a sense of shared values (what is "non-negotiable" in how they do business), and operating practices (how things really get done) that are compatible with our purpose, values, and beliefs.

So, how would you define your personal PURPOSE according to this definition? To what degree is your personal PURPOSE aligned with the organization/opportunity in question? 3 = Great Fit, 2 = OK Fit, 1 = Poor/Partial Fit, 0 = Not a Fit, DK = Don't Know/Not Sure

Level 2: PASSION

Within our chosen vocation, there are likely to be certain types of work we find particularly interesting. Furthermore, we are likely to have a point of view (philosophy) about the best approach, focus, and outcomes to be achieved by that work. Ideally, the mission of any organization, its vision of success, the strategies it is committed to achieving, and the philosophies to which it ascribes, should not only be interesting but should engender a certain passion within us. A strong passion and interest in the work are critical to our long-term fulfillment and to bringing our very best self to work.

So, how would you define your PASSION according to this definition? To what degree is your PASSION aligned with the organization/opportunity in question? 3 = Great Fit, 2 = OK Fit, 1 = Poor/Partial Fit, 0 = Not a Fit, DK = Don't Know/Not Sure

Level 3: PROFICIENCY

Each of us brings certain professional competencies, skills, and experience to the workplace, and to any specific role we occupy. Thus, we will inherently demonstrate varying degrees of proficiency and effectiveness in our work. However, of equal importance is the degree to which we enjoy and are motivated to engage in certain of our proficiencies. These are thought of as our "motivated" proficiencies or abilities. Conversely, the organization has certain expectations regarding our ability to demonstrate proficiency to do the work and achieve the goals of the role we occupy.

So, how would you define your "motivated" PROFICIENCIES according to this definition? To what degree are your "motivated" PROFICIENCIES aligned with the organization/opportunity in question?

3 = Great Fit, 2 = OK Fit, 1 = Poor/Partial Fit, 0 = Not a Fit, DK = Don't Know/Not Sure

Level 4: PREFERENCES

Every person possesses a specific personality and temperament. As such, we are naturally most comfortable and motivated in environments that are compatible with how we are wired personally. In turn, the organization also has a certain "personality." For example, the environment may be highly energetic, extroverted, and fast-paced or more introverted, steady, methodical, and so forth. In addition, we may respond differently to certain types of leadership and management styles and approaches, which could positively or negatively affect our level of motivation, ownership, and commitment to the job and the organization.

So, how would you define your PREFERENCES according to this definition? To what degree are your PREFERENCES aligned with the organization/opportunity in question? 3 = Great Fit, 2 = OK Fit, 1 = Poor/Partial Fit, 0 = Not a Fit, DK = Don't Know/Not Sure

Level 5: PERSONAL NEEDS

While our vocation may be very important to us, we each have certain personal needs and wants related to other areas of our life. Therefore, both the expectations of the organization and the benefits that accrue to us from our work should be compatible with our life goals and our lifestyle needs and wants. Current compensation, long-term financial opportunity, health benefits, work schedule and location, travel requirements, and time off are examples of areas where our needs must be in alignment with the provisions and expectations of the organization.

So, how would you define your PERSONAL NEEDS according to this definition? To what degree are your PERSONAL NEEDS aligned with the organization/opportunity in question? 3 = Great Fit, 2 = OK Fit, 1 = Poor/Partial Fit, 0 = Not a Fit, DK = Don't Know/Not Sure

Level 6: PICTURE OF SUCCESS

Each of us has potential for professional growth beyond our current (or proposed) role. As such, we each have (or should have) a vision or picture of where we would like to take our career long-term. To fully realize this career potential and picture of success, we will need certain kinds of developmental experiences, job assignments, and leadership opportunities along the way. Therefore, we should not only ensure alignment with the organization concerning our current (or proposed) role, but we should also be certain how the organization can (and will) provide the kind of support we need to advance our careers toward the achievement of our long-term potential.

So, how would you define your PICTURE OF SUCCESS according to this definition? To what degree is your PICTURE OF SUCCESS aligned with the organization/opportunity in question? 3 = Great Fit, 2 = OK Fit, 1 = Poor/Partial Fit, 0 = Not a Fit, DK = Don't Know/Not Sure

6 P Career Development Conversations

3 = Great Fit, 2 = OK Fit, 1 = Poor/Partial Fit, 0 = Not a Fit, DK = Don't Know/Not Sure

YOU		ORGANIZATION	
Level 1: *PURPOSE* Sense of Purpose / Values / Beliefs		Purpose / Values / Guiding Principles	
Level 2: *PASSION* Passions / Interests / Point of View		Mission / Vision / Strategy / Philosophy	
Level 3: *PROFICIENCY* Motivated Abilities / Skills		Work / Role / Job Goals	
Level 4: *PREFERENCE* Personality / Motivators		Environment / Culture / Leadership Style	
Level 5: *PERSONAL NEEDS* Lifestyle Requirements		Comp / Benefits / Work Schedule	
Level 6: *PICTURE OF SUCCESS* Career & Leadership Goals		Career Development Opportunity	

Discussion Questions:

- As you think about the future, what are your long-term goals? (Note: This question is intentionally open-ended and responses may range from personal to family to community to financial to spiritual to vocational. Invite but don't force sharing!)

- When you consider these goals together, where would you ideally like to be in your job/career in five years?
- What do you feel are your greatest strengths (skills, competencies, personal characteristics) in achieving that vision for your career?
- In what areas (skills, competencies, personal characteristics) do feel you need to change or grow in order to achieve that vision for your career?
- What responsibilities or conditions in your current job role do you personally find most satisfying and/or rewarding?
- What responsibilities or conditions in your current job role do you find least satisfying and/or rewarding?
- If you could design the job you would love to do right now, what would it look like?
  > What responsibilities would it include?
  > What service or value would you provide to others and the organization?
  > What would the working environment around you be like?
- What other information would you like us/me to know as we/I continue to think about our organization and your role in it… both now and in the future?

MISSIONAL - Legacy Impact – Life Purpose

Guiding principles regarding…**Legacy Impact – Purpose**

- A clear and written purpose is vital to achieve a lasting impact and leave a legacy.
- Clarity of purpose leads to priorities that help one take action.

The Power of Purpose – Writing your Life Purpose Statement

Answers the "Why" of your life in order to hear "Well done, good and faithful servant."

*"He knows the 'why' for his existence and will be able to bear almost any 'how.'" — **Viktor Frankl, holocaust survivor***

"One never really lives unless he has something to die for" — **Søren Kierkegaard**

"Life is Short – Make every day count" – Faithful to opportunity.

"It is easy to make a fortune, it is very hard to make a difference." We all will give an account of how we spent our lives. The question is, were we faithful to our purpose. We have a choice. A lack of purpose leads to: Frustration, Busyness, Discontentment, Regret. There are significant and eternal rewards to knowing and living out your purpose.

1. Hope and Motivation
2. Joy and Contentment
3. Peace and Security
4. Significance and Satisfaction
5. Fruit and a Legacy
6. Reward and Recognition

Life Purpose Statement "It is not about you." Rick Warren			
Why	**Why is it important? Two hundred years from now, what impact will your life make?**		
	Questions	**Reflections, Ideas, Thoughts, Heart**	**One Word**
	What are your life dreams and priorities that are beyond you? What lasting difference would you like to see in your life? What do you instinctively take action on? What frustrates you or causes you concern in this world?		
Who	**Who do you serve? Who are you willing to sacrifice for?**		
	Who do you do it for? Who are you helping improve or grow? Is it others-oriented?		
What	**What actions do you take? What are you good at that will help others?**		

	What do you love to do? What is the one thing you can truly teach someone else? What action is in your design? What makes you feel alive? What are your passions, gifts, strengths, and skills?		
How	**How do others change? How will this action make a difference?**		
	What do they want or need? How do they transform as a result of what you give them? What good works will it accomplish?		
Life Purpose Statement:			
2-3 Word Purpose:			

Chapter Twelve

CONCLUSION

The following are observations from the book *It's the Manager* by Jim Clifton and Jim Harter.

It's the Manager: Gallup Finds the Quality of Managers and Team Leaders is the Single Biggest Factor in Your Organization's Long-Term Success.

Gallup recommends that organizations immediately change their cultures. These are the six biggest changes that we discovered:

1. Millennials and Generation Z don't just work for a paycheck—they want a purpose. For people in these generations, their work must have meaning. They want to work for organizations with a mission and purpose. In the past, baby boomers and other generations didn't necessarily need meaning in their jobs. They just wanted a paycheck. Their mission and purpose were their families and communities. For millennials and Generation Z, compensation is important and must be fair, but it's no longer their primary motivation. The emphasis for these generations has switched from paycheck to purpose—and so should your culture.

2. Millennials and Generation Z are no longer pursuing job satisfaction; they are pursuing development. Most members of these generations don't care about the bells and whistles in many workplaces today—the ping-pong tables, fancy latte machines, and free food that companies offer to try to create job satisfaction. Giving

out toys and entitlements is a leadership mistake. And worse, it's condescending.

3. Millennials and Generation Z don't want bosses—they want coaches. The role of an old-style boss is command and control. But millennials and Generation Z care about having team leaders who can coach them, who value them as individuals and employees, and who help them understand and build their strengths.

4. Millennials and Generation Z don't want annual reviews—they want ongoing conversations. How these generations communicate—texting, tweeting, Skype, etc.—is immediate and continuous. Millennials and Generation Z are accustomed to constant communication and feedback, and this dramatically affects the workplace. Annual reviews on their own have never worked.

5. Millennials and Generation Z don't want a manager who fixates on their weaknesses. Gallup research shows that weaknesses never develop into strengths, while strengths develop infinitely. Your organization should not ignore weaknesses. Rather, you should understand weaknesses but maximize strengths. A strengths-based culture also helps you attract and keep star team members.

6. It's not my job—it's my life. As we noted earlier, one of Gallup's discoveries is that what everyone in the world wants is a good job. This is especially true for millennials and Generation Z. More so than ever in the history of corporate culture, employees are asking, "Does this organization value my strengths and my contribution? Does this organization give me the chance to do what I do best every day?" For millennials and Generation Z, a job is no longer just a job—it's their life.

Conclusion from Gallup

Reposition your managers as coaches. Only your best managers can implement the culture you want. A great culture is one of the few things an organization can't buy. Managers at all levels make or break your culture change. And traditional performance management systems have struggled to inspire and develop employees, which can result in billions of dollars in lost productivity. **Today's employees want a coach, not a boss.** Moving your managers from boss to coach not only increases employee engagement and improves performance, but it's also essential to changing your culture.

As you become a Coaching Leader, your influence, impact, and satisfaction will grow, and you will have a positive effect on many people's lives. The process takes time, yet the rewards are overwhelming.

Make a commitment to yourself to enter into this process. Take time to learn and then apply the principles and best practices. Seek out a coach who is down the road from you to learn and grow with.

Be ready for a life-changing adventure in your leadership!

CONCLUSION

ABOUT THE AUTHOR

Bruce R. Witt is President of Leadership Revolution Inc., a non-profit organization dedicated to developing and multiplying servant leaders to reach their world. He began his career in marketing for Shell Oil Company in the solid plastics area. He was led to join the Christian Business Men's Committee where he directed the U.S. field operations and authored several key curriculum for the ministry, including the Operation Timothy spiritual development series and the Lighthouse evangelism curriculum.

In 2008, after seeing the tremendous need for leaders to understand and practice successful leadership principles, Bruce was led to form Leadership Revolution in order to establish a process that would help leaders.

Bruce has written curriculum and training resources and he regularly travels throughout the United States and the globe conducting workshops, conferences and train the trainer sessions to spread the vision and empower others. Along with partner organizations and churches, Bruce has trained thousands of leaders and trained hundreds of trainers who can also train others.

Bruce has been married to his wife Dana for 40 years and they have two grown sons—Robert, married to Allison, and Andrew, married to Amy, who have three sons: Brooks, Harrison, and Cooper.

THE BROADER PLAN FOR YOUR LEADERSHIP DEVELOPMENT

In this inspiring and practical book, *SERVE–The Five Disciplines of Great Leadership*, Bruce Witt clearly guides all leaders through the following areas of servant leadership –

- The Foundation of Servant Leadership
- The 5-part SERVE Model to lead as a servant
- The 5 GREAT Actions that help you apply the SERVE Model
- Helpful tips and resources to share with your team

ISBN 978-0-9965714-2-5
176 pages, Softcover

Life is full of ups and downs, encouragements and challenges, and the one thing that will help us not only survive but thrive is our attitude. *The Power of Attitude: Eight Perspectives That Will Change Your World* will help you impact your personal world and extend your influence to the entire world. By learning the eight attitudes that frame your life journey, you can radically change and make a lasting difference in your purpose and outlook.

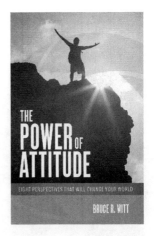

ISBN 978-0-9965714-7-0
104 pages, Softcover